Branded Bodies, Rhetoric,
and the Neoliberal Nation-State

Cultural Studies/Pedagogy/Activism

Series Editors:
Rachel Riedner, The George Washington University
Randi Gray Kristensen, The George Washington University

Advisory Board:

Paul Apostolidis, Whitman College; Rebecca Dingo, University of Missouri; Byron Hawk, University of South Carolina; Susan Jarratt, University of California, Irvine; David Kellogg, Coastal Carolina University; Kevin Mahoney, Kutztown University; Robert McRuer, The George Washington University; Dan Moshenberg, The George Washington University; Pegeen Reichert Powell, Columbia College; April Shemak, Sam Houston State University.

The Lexington Books **Cultural Studies/Pedagogy/Activism** series offers books that engage with questions about the intersection of contemporary cultural studies, critical pedagogy, and activism. Anticipating interdisciplinary audiences, books in the series aim to interrogate and inform pedagogical practice and activism with theoretical concerns from cultural studies, feminism, political theory and economy, rhetoric and composition, postcolonial theory, U.S. ethnic and transnational studies, and more.

Titles in the Series

Democracies to Come: Rhetorical Action, Neoliberalism, and Communities of Resistance, by Rachel Riedner and Kevin Mahoney

Writing Against the Curriculum: Anti-Disciplinarity in the Writing and Cultural Studies Classroom, edited by Randi Gray Kristensen and Ryan M. Claycomb

Gramsci, Language, and Translation, edited by Peter Ives and Rocco Lacorte

Rhetorics for Community Action: Public Writing and Writing Publics, by Phyllis Mentzell Ryder

Teaching Writing in Globalization: Remapping Disciplinary Work, edited by Darin Payne and Daphne Desser

Circulating Communities: The Tactics and Strategies of Community Publishing, edited by Paula Mathie, Steve Parks, and Tiffany Rousculp

Unsustainable: Owning our Best, Short-Lived Efforts as Community Work, edited by Laurie Cella and Jessica Restaino

Branded Bodies, Rhetoric, and the Neoliberal Nation-State

Jennifer Wingard

LEXINGTON BOOKS
Lanham • Boulder • New York • Toronto • Plymouth, UK

Published by Lexington Books
A wholly owned subsidiary of The Rowman & Littlefield Publishing Group, Inc.
4501 Forbes Boulevard, Suite 200, Lanham, Maryland 20706
www.rowman.com

10 Thornbury Road, Plymouth PL6 7PP, United Kingdom

British Library Cataloguing in Publication Information Available

Library of Congress Cataloging-in-Publication Data
Wingard, Jennifer, 1975-
Branded bodies, rhetoric, and the neoliberal nation-state / Jennifer Wingard.
p. cm. — (Cultural studies/pedagogy/activism)
Includes bibliographical references and index.
ISBN 978-0-7391-8020-4 (cloth : alk. paper) — ISBN 978-0-7391-8021-1 (electronic)
1. Human body—Social aspects. 2. Human body—Political aspects. 3. Human body—Symbolic aspects. 4. Neoliberalism. I. Title.
GT495.W56 2013
306.4—dc23
2012043571

Printed in the United States of America

Table of Contents

Acknowledgments

This book began with a memory. It was the memory of my grandmother Virginia Escabado Brandes telling me that she had a hard life because, ever since she arrived in the United States at five years old, she "never felt comfortable or understood by anyone she met. [She] always felt strange." When I was an angst-ridden twelve-year-old, her sentiment made complete existential sense—after all, how could anyone really know anyone else? But as I grew up and learned the realities involved in the life of a long-term Mexican immigrant, I began to want to more fully understand the uneasiness my grandmother carried with her.

So I thank Virginia for her honesty in telling her granddaughter not about the hardships she encountered growing up away from her family, as a displaced Mestiza from Zacatecas living in Beverly Hills, nor for spinning a narrative of overcoming her immigrant past, while living two blocks from the beach and managing property in one of California's most exclusive neighborhoods. Instead, I thank her for talking to me about how her past *affected* her, because from that simple statement, this book was born.

But there were many more who influenced and helped me move this book from concept to concrete object. Much of the research for the project was done during my graduate work at Syracuse University, and it was there that I was fortunate enough to have several mentors who engaged with my questions, concerns, and grandiose ideas about immigration, GLBT rights, Marxism, feminism, and critical race theory. Both Linda Martín Alcoff and Chandra Talpade Mohanty were instrumental in pushing me to better understand how power functions across the globe and throughout inceptions of identity. Margaret Himley, Lois Agnew, Robin Riley, Collin Brooke, Gwen Pough, and Vivian May were all willing to engage with me during the early stages of my work. Their willingness to listen while I wandered through complex ideas allowed me to better develop as a thinker and writer. Eileen Schell helped ground the project in multiple fields by pushing me to clearly articulate the deep connections I saw between transnational feminism and rhetoric. Additionally, Eileen, Linda, and Chandra served as mentors to and advocates for me numerous times, thus routinely embodying feminism.

As the project continued to grow, I received support from my colleagues at the University of Houston. Jim Zebroski and Paul Butler are not only the best colleagues with whom to build a graduate program, but they are also staunch intellectuals who are willing to listen, mentor, and provide feedback on any aspect of faculty work. For their interest and support, I am continually grateful. I am also thankful for the interested and engaged graduate students at the University of Houston, especially Brandon Hernsberger and Michelle Miley. Brandon and Michelle both have read and responded to drafts of this work, and their insight and intellectual exchange only made the work stronger. Finally, I want to thank the University of Houston New Faculty Grant Program for providing funding during the development of this project, and the Martha Gano Houstoun Fund and the University of Houston Small Grants Program for providing monetary support for the production of this book.

Scholarship is labor, first and foremost, and none of us labor in isolation. *Branded Bodies* would not be nearly as strong a text without the invaluable advice and feedback of Rachel Riedner and Rebecca Dingo. Since the three of us met in 2007, we bonded over similar scholarly and personal endeavors. I cannot stress how important their feedback and friendship is to me. The same sentiment could be said for my partner Michael Sicinski, who has read and edited almost every version of this book. Of his scholarly acumen, kind heart, and pedantic grammatical eye, I am forever in awe.

Even though this book is, in many ways, a testament to my grandmother Virginia, it is also a testament to my family. Both the Brandeses and the Delgados have experienced a fraught history with their Mexican heritage, yet no family member has ever spoken of my work with anything but love and support. Additionally, they have provided monetary (at times) and domestic (quite often) support when I have needed to travel or work into the evenings or on weekends. Lee and Linda, Fran and Mike, I thank you for all that you have given through the years.

Finally, I would like to dedicate this book to my daughter, Nola Virginia. She was never able to meet her great-grandmother, but she carries her name forward. I hope that the work I do here enables her to do so in a world where all people are assured dignity and understanding by the governments who are bound to serve them. *Te amo, hija. Mi libro es por tu.*

Preface

Branding Bodies: Assembling Affective Responses

Branded Bodies, Rhetoric, and the Neoliberal Nation-State explores how neoliberal economics has affected the rhetoric of the media and politics, and how in very direct, material ways it harms the bodies of some of the United States's most vulnerable occupants. This book is written in a neoliberal moment when the promise of the liberal nation-state, one in which the government purports to care for its citizens through social welfare programs financed by state funds, is eroding. Currently, state policies are defined by neoliberal governmentality that privileges privatization of government industry and individual personal responsibility. Therefore, instead of the promise of citizenship and the protections that come with it, "the American Dream" (to use a common euphemism), the state uses certain bodies that will never be accepted as citizens as an underclass in service of capital (think "Guest Worker Programs"). And those underclassed "bodies" are identified through branding.

Branding of bodies and the assembling of those brands work to turn "others" into rhetorical products, much like consummable products in advertising. Those products, then, are circulated and used to establish a core national identity in a time of economic and political flux. Part of the reason branding works is because it creates an object upon which the American public can focus their emotions. Branding redirects the anxieties that the material conditions of neoliberal capital produce through unemployment, economic disenfranchisement, and changing demographics. *Branded Bodies* shows how both media and governmental rhetorical outlets have made immigrant and GLBT[1] citizen bodies into "brands" that serve as cautionary tales of what to avoid, whom to fear, and who is outside the norm of citizenship. And because their bodies have been made into brands, GLBT people and immigrants are evacuated of any human characteristics and turned into threatening "things" from which citizens need protection. Threatening attributes are stuck to these bodies and circulated, firming up and establishing a racialized and gendered national identity.

Branding, then, is not merely a rhetorical strategy. It is an affective one as well. In the case of branding, language is not merely a means to persuade, although it can be very persuasive. Instead, brands serve to create emotions through identification with images and symbols, and those

emotions circulate, as discussed by Sara Ahmed in "Affective Economies," gaining value depending on their context and intelligibility. In
other words, branding is a rhetorical strategy that focuses on pathos rather than logos, in the traditional sense. And it is our association with the
emotional effects of branding that makes particular brands more or less
valuable. Brands do not "argue" positions; they work to enable certain
debates and arguments through compelling emotion. For that reason,
brands become quite powerful in national discourse.

In order to demonstrate just how influential branding and the assembling of brands has become, I offer readings of key pieces of legislation on
immigration and GLBT rights and their media reception from the past
twenty years. By alternating between legal and media documents, I will
show the centrality of branding to neoliberal politics. Many rhetorical
scholars (Jenny Rice, Wendy Hesford, Rebecca Dingo) have argued that
focusing on one particular rhetorical situation, text, or location cannot
account for the complex exchanges of context and/or power present in
current rhetorical production. I draw in particular upon Dingo's articulation of networking to demonstrate how rhetoricians can "articulate the
complex ways that the rhetorical appeals reach a diffused yet linked audience, while also accounting for how contiguous power relationships
add meaning and force to arguments" (Dingo 486). Articulating how
contiguous texts invoke uneven power relationships by drawing on historical and cultural assumptions is key to the work of *Branded Bodies*. To
do so, I use *assemblage* as a method of conjoining and reading texts which
are not traditionally placed in conversation with one another.

By assembling a critique of branding and how brands are assembled
to create affective threats, I will demonstrate both how dangerous the
branding of bodies has become, as well as how we might begin to repair
the damage or craft political responses by materially assembling the histories and economic realities of those bodies. Assembling brands, histories, or political narratives in nontraditional ways can form counter-narratives that challenge dominant brands. In chapter five, I focus on the
productive power of the assemblage by arguing for a re-assembling of
the brand "worker" instead of a mere re-branding. It is through a recon-
figuration of the histories and associations that undergird national understandings of work that a true political response can be crafted. Therefore,
assemblage as a method allows for political responses to be created
through *contiguous* connections between bodies, histories, and power,
rather than *causal* ones. Because of that, the assemblage can be a powerful
rhetorical method of production and critique.

Assemblage is not only the method used in this book; it also is a
means to combine brands to further disenfranchise certain bodies. Assemblage can work to combine affective characteristics of brands by allowing the features of those brands to begin to "stick," to use Sara Ahmed's term, to one another. For example, in chapter three, I discuss how

Immigration and Customs Enforcement (ICE) polices immigrant, GLBT, and other "bodies" by allowing each brand to affectively influence others. These brands are then used to build an image of a united and protected nation-state in a time of economic and political uncertainty. However, because the assemblage is a practice that is about process and connectivity rather than analogy and causality, the assemblage does not create fixed iterations. Instead, it has the ability to create multiple iterations and meanings depending on context, much like Dingo's discussion of networked rhetorics. The work of the book, then, is to contextualize and define the use of brands made about GLBT and immigrant bodies. And to offer an alternative rhetorical practice that can begin to challenge the work that branding has done over the past thirty years.

THE WORK OF *BRANDED BODIES*

The work of *Branded Bodies* is an intervention into rhetorical and political (meaning state and economic power) practice. The exigency of this work is the current moment of global economic crisis that is marked by market crashes, high levels of national debt and default, and increasing unemployment rates. Although these conditions can be found worldwide, I will concentrate on the U.S. government's responses as exemplary of the shift from liberal to neoliberal governmentality. In a liberal model of governmentality (government's claim is that they care for and protect populations), there is an expectation that governments will intervene in economic crises. Governments have intervened in recent economic "crashes," but their support has gone directly to corporate interests and bank accounts, not directly to corporate workers or state citizens. This practice marks a shift in liberal governmentality. As I will show more specifically in chapter one, the state is no longer economically invested in the support of its citizens. Instead, we see government bailouts targeting large corporate interest based on the theory that profits will "trickle down" to the masses.

This is a move to neoliberal governmentality where the states across the globe progressively shift their own monetary investments in national programs and jobs toward the support of the free market, and as such, corporate privatization becomes the norm both economically and politically. According to Gilles Deleuze, these shifts mark the weakening of public control of institutions such as the "prison, hospital, factory, school and family" ("Society of Control"). But instead of those institutions transparently morphing into new forms of governance, Deleuze claims, "[t]he administrations in charge never cease announcing supposedly necessary reforms" ("Postscript Society of Control"). Deleuze speaks of the privatization of social services, but he also makes note that instead of announcing the shift of control as such, states rely on the language of crisis to obfuscate this transfer. Deleuze sees the gap between the material reality of state privatization and the language of its representation as an ideologically seamless one. The economic policy and political ideology of neoliberalism blend so completely that it seems as if they are naturally one and the same feature of "the neoliberal condition" (to paraphrase Lyotard). In other words, Deleuze demonstrates how the rhetoric of crisis does not truly denote economic crises. Instead, it is allowing for a mystification of the lack of state involvement in citizens' private lives. He claims that the rhetoric of crisis is intrinsic to neoliberal privatization, but I would argue that the privatization of social services and the rhetoric of crisis that occludes the state's responsibility are examples of what Rebecca Dingo calls "neoliberal logics" (*Networking Arguments* 7), or what Aihwa Ong refers to as "neoliberal technologies" (*Neoliberalism as Exception* 5).

These "logics" and "technologies" are the rhetorical features and material processes that undergird the transition from liberal to neoliberal governmentality. For Dingo, a "logic" is a seemingly universal set of assumptions that are constructed within a particular historical, economic, and national site. In other words, a logic helps to forward economic and material conditions by linking in a seemingly inevitable manner sustained and known ideologies. For Ong, a "technology" is the undergirding process(es) in which a logic becomes a logic. For her, a technology can be any practice which allows for the forwarding of a particular ideology. Ong implores us to look at neoliberalism not as an overarching ideology, but rather as a set of practices or technologies (for example, privatization and rhetoric of personal responsibility) in order to understand how it can become a universalizing feature of a nation or transnational network. In other words, Ong calls for a more nuanced understanding of how neoliberal economics and the spread of regulatory power to individuals and corporations impact the claims and definitions that states can make on behalf of and about citizens.

Branded Bodies argues that branding is a technology that serves neoliberal governmentality. As such, it is central to the construction of a seemingly unified national identity formed in response to the shift from liberal governmentality to state policies dictated by neoliberal economics. In order to make visible the material and ideological connections that branding of bodies mystifies, I draw on transnational feminism, cultural studies, and rhetorical and political theory. Each of the theorists I engage from these fields—Jasbir Puar, Sara Ahmed, Aihwa Ong, J. Blake Scott, Rebecca Dingo, Rachel Riedner, Alan Arvidsson, and Jodi Dean—focuses on the material consequences and context of neoliberal economics. Yet each different scholarly approach allows me to combine multiple views on the theories of neoliberalism, circulation, and identification. Through the combination of these fields, I can demonstrate how neoliberal economics is not only a political and economic shift, but also a cultural and affective one.

Chapter one focuses on the historical, economic, and theoretical underpinnings of neoliberalism that *Branded Bodies* engages. The theoretical work in this chapter grounds the discussions throughout the book. Therefore, instead of defining a general context of neoliberalism, this book instead focuses on how Aihwa Ong's notion of neoliberalism as exception has permeated our ideas of nationality and citizenship over the past twenty years. Coupling that with Jodi Dean's discussion of the anxieties produced by the dissolution of state-run institutions, I show how branding of bodies is used to stimulate emotions and forward the image of a unified nation-state. It is the bodies of GLBT people and immigrants that are branded to support that unified vision. Chapter one engages the link between the circulation of emotions and brands as a means to explain how GLBT and immigrant bodies become the site of nation-building in a time of national economic crisis.

Chapter two more fully articulates the use of immigrants and GLBT bodies as brands that represent internal and external threats to the nation-state. This chapter looks at legislation that attempts to determine who can be a family and who cannot—primarily H.R. 4437 and the Defense of Marriage Act (DOMA). Within the logic of this legislation, the primary figure at risk is the American family; it is the immigrant body that will intrude and break into the family from outside and the GLBT body that will deceive and disrupt the family from the inside. These threats are complementary, but seldom seen as corollary. The successful implementation of the brands is due in large part to the ways they draw on histories of racism, misogyny, and sexism that have come to be normalized as part of our national imagery. By assembling different pieces of key legislation and the media responses to them, we can see how the branding of the family is forwarded as a means to evoke emotional reactions that engage questions of protection and what it means to be American.

In chapter three, I explore the material consequences of the assemblage. I look at both the Patriot Act of 2001 and the development of Immigration and Customs Enforcement (ICE), which is the law enforcement arm of Homeland Security. I argue that ICE is the material manifestation of the rhetorical assemblage because it not only assembles brands and rhetorical representations of threats, but it is a law enforcement umbrella that monitors immigration, computer fraud, sexual predators, and missing persons (to name but a few duties). As a law enforcement agency that polices both immigrants and sex offenders, ICE is the culmination of a branding process wherein all threats become devoid of their material and historical specificities. Instead, each crime becomes, at best, equivalent; at worst, each category of crime becomes imbued with the characteristics of the other crimes policed by ICE.

Chapter four discusses the danger of these rhetorical and material assemblages by analyzing the case of José Padilla, who is stripped of his humanity and designated an "enemy combatant," and the assassination of Osama bin Laden. When bodies are branded they become "bare life" — bodies without any political or social identity in the eyes of the nation-state (Agamben 4). By showing this, I argue that as scholars we must take measures to resist this kind of branding and assembling by connecting state and media rhetoric to the material conditions and bodies they describe. Bin Laden's assassination demonstrates the collision between the brand and the body of "bin Laden" through his death. It is this incommensurability, I argue, that has created all the evasion and confusion surrounding his death.

Finally, chapter five examines the figure of the worker in order to show how assemblage can operate as an alternative reading practice. I argue that although "worker" has been used as a brand, such as in the development of the Employment Non-discrimination Act (ENDA), it can also serve to reconnect bodies with the humanity that branding has stripped from them. This chapter looks at both the development of ENDA and the May Day rallies of 2006–2010 to show how assemblage can function as a positive rhetorical and activist strategy when the narratives are drawn together in consideration *of* power, not *within* power.

Branded Bodies is an intervention into the rhetorical practices of the nation-state as it attempts to clarify *how* the nation-state uses brands and branding to forward its claims of equality and freedom, while at the same time condemning those who do not "fit in" to particular categories valued by the neoliberal state. Ultimately, branding leads to the utter dehumanization of marginalized people. It enables the state to imprison and mentally abandon citizens like José Padilla and assassinate enemies of the state, such as Osama bin Laden. *Branded Bodies* not only focuses on the ways that media, government agencies, and even the law itself work together to dehumanize targeted groups through branding and rhetorical assemblage, but also focuses on how those moves toward branding and rhetorical assemblage mystify the material economic and political downturns of global neoliberal economics facing U.S. citizens.

NOTES

1. I have chosen to use GLBT as the modifier to denote Gay, Lesbian, Bisexual, and Transgendered instead of LGBT or LGBTQ throughout the book because, within discussions of gay and lesbian rights in the U.S. media, GLBT is the most common acronym. One reason for this may be, as Lisa Duggan discussed in a post-talk Q & A at the University of Houston, GLBT places Gay and Lesbian first (GL) and sublimates the bisexual and transgendered (BT), therefore giving preference to more "recognizable and accepted (even if alternative) lifestyle choices" ("Imperial Dreams").

ONE

Othering and Branding

Assembling Neoliberal Identities

WHY BRANDING?

This chapter looks at how material "terms" (according to Duggan), "others" (according to Ahmed), or "brands" (according to this book) are used within the context of neoliberalism, and also how they are used to solidify the power of the nation-state. It attempts to assemble a series of key terms (such as "others," "other-others," "exceptions," and "imagined communities") to demonstrate how these terms work together to affectively produce the material conditions under which branding becomes a central rhetorical technology of neoliberalism. In neoliberal rhetoric, it may seem as if the nation-state is behaving rationally by offering "free markets" and "limitless opportunity," but as Duggan, Ong, Ahmed, and others demonstrate, that opportunity is available only to those who fall into appropriate and accepted citizenship categories. The access to those categories is being regulated through capital, and these terms have become commodities themselves through the branding of others. This chapter, then, explains how and why the nation-state uses brands to forward its claims of equality and freedom while it simultaneously condemns those who do not fit into particular categories valued by the neoliberal state.

In addition, this chapter will explain how branding functions both rhetorically and affectively. First, I will discuss how neoliberalism as a form of exception creates the conditions wherein certain groups become targets for branding. Next, I will frame branding in its material, economic and governmental context. From there, I will discuss how branding functions as a false remedy to particular social anxieties arising from neoliberal practices. In discussions of the shift from a disciplinary society to a society of control, it has been noted that this evolution has created an affective need for branding and assemblage in cultural and national identity formation. Finally, I will demonstrate why understanding both branding and assemblage as rhetorical processes can provide a means to intervene in detrimental and non-material neoliberal rhetorical practices.

NEOLIBERALISM *AS* EXCEPTION: THE PRIVATE MADE PUBLIC

In the spring of 2010, Texas Rep. Debbie Riddle proposed House Bill (H.B.) 2012, which sought to fine or imprison employers who "intentionally, knowingly, or recklessly hire" undocumented immigrants.[1] It was not these stipulations that caught media attention, however. It was the exemption Rep. Riddle included in the Bill, which stated that employers hiring undocumented workers were in violation of state law "unless they were hiring a maid, a lawn care worker, or another houseworker" (Castillo). Many supporters of the bill said the exemption was necessary, especially in Texas. As Democratic Rep. Aaron Pena told CNN, "With things as they are today, her bill will see a large segment of the Texas population in prison if it passes without the exception."[2] (Castillo). Others saw the exemption as a necessary intervention because the continued hiring of undocumented domestic workers helps sustain the Texas economy.

Although many throughout Texas viewed the exception included in H.B. 2012 as a site-specific response to exception-less Senate Bill (S.B.) 1070,[3] which had passed in Arizona a year earlier, I see the exception as indicative of neoliberal shifts in the discourses of citizenship in the United States. The key feature of neoliberalism as exception is the marked change by which the clearly defined rules and regulations (and benefits) regarding citizenship have begun to shift in answer to the needs of capital. Instead of citizenship being a clear outcome for those who follow the procedures set forth by host countries, there are now regulations defining groups based on their documented, but non-citizenship status (for example, "guest workers" and "student visas," which I discuss at length in chapter five). These "exceptions" to the procedures of citizenship reveal that certain classes of bodies enter the country solely to support capital and do not gain rights in the eyes of the nation-state.

These exceptions to U.S. citizenship and immigration law, like the one clearly articulated in H.B. 2012, reveal the deep ties to the rhetoric of *personal responsibility* and the economic policies of privatization that undergird discussions of immigration. "Neoliberal decisions have created new forms of inclusion, setting apart some citizen-subjects, and creating new spaces that enjoy extraordinary political benefits and economic gain" (Ong 5).[4] Aihwa Ong draws on the example of Free Trade Zones (FTZ) wherein low-wage immigrants are subject to regulation not by the state, but instead by corporate and economic policy. She also reminds us of expatriate and immigrant elites who attain visas through their connection to particular global institutions, corporations, universities and/or state agencies which allow for citizenship-like status, though it is never required that they become full citizens. The subjects afforded these exceptions are never seen as "full citizens" within these zones, but they are given rights approximating citizenship because of their class-status and desirability to capital. In other words, these exceptions work to give rights to those who should not have them because it is in the best interest of capital to do so.

But the exceptions to citizenship can be seen working within the borders of the United States as a means to define citizenship during a time when FTZs, expatriate relocation, and student university visas are generating questions and anxieties about who is acceptable within our national borders and who is not. Part of my argument is that just as neoliberal exceptionalism is a global phenomenon, it is a central logic of U.S. neoliberal governmentality as well. Part of the success of strict immigration laws, such as Arizona's S.B. 1070 and Alabama's House Bill (H.B.) 56,[5] which place stiff penalties on employers who hire undocumented workers and also allow law enforcement agents to inquire about immigration documentation during routine traffic stops or other minor violations, is that they create a means of policing immigrants solely based on their perceived documentation status. There need not be a civil or criminal trial; instead, documentation violations are enough to deem these immigrants criminals. Many critics and supporters alike argue over the ability to actually enforce these laws fairly, but for this project, what is more crucial is what these laws reveal about borders and boundaries of U.S. citizenship.

S.B. 1070 and H.B. 56 demonstrate the difficulties present in defining the terms of immigration and citizenship in a neoliberal world. As the U.S. nation-state continues to cede its regulatory power in favor of corporate self-regulation and municipal control, the definitions of citizenship and immigrant status are effected. As a result, "Myriad disarticulations and rearticulations occasioned by the logic of the exception transform the elements we used to associate with a unified concept of citizenship into values placed on humanity that are increasingly varied, fragmented, contingent, and ambiguous" (Ong 27). Therefore, discussions of citizenship have begun to focus on features of citizenship that are contextual, shifting, and unstable, rather than state mandated "rights," because of the precarious nature of the state. Nation-states and public discourse begin to define citizenship through community or national values that benefit the national myth of a unified economy and identity.

The neoliberal complications present in defining citizenship are evident, too, in Texas's H.B. 2012. However, we see complications not through the types of draconian measures present in Arizona or Alabama, but through the exception. By placing particular exceptions into the bill allowing for only certain employers and workers to be deemed "dangerous" to the Texas economy while creating a link between other "acceptable" or "non-threatening" workers and our domestic lives, Texas legislators reestablish and assume the feminized docility and non-resistant nature of domestic workers and domestic space,[6] at the same time as they reify the intimate sphere of neoliberal privatization that is well established in Texas. In the rhetoric of the bill, the private employers and employees (regardless of their immigration status) should not be held to the same rules as those employers operating what are considered to be public work sites (for example, construction sites, corporate workplaces, or any workplace that is not a home). H.B. 2012 thus reified the gendered division of labor in Texas wherein there are two kinds of labor and two kinds of employers—public and private.

This differentiation between sites of labor provides a narrative about Texas's commitment to private interest over statewide mandates, practices, or laws. The private citizen and his/her home are central to both the ideologies and economic policies that structure Texas life.[7] It is because of these policies that Texas becomes an exemplary site to discuss how aspects of privatization—a feature central of the economic and political practices of neoliberalism—tell stories about who the American public "others" and who is exempted from this othering in order to define the national public as discrete communities—homeowners, Texans, Americans. Furthermore, the rhetoric of personal responsibility and the pursuit of economic self-interest demonstrate the clear logic of neoliberalism (Dingo 15), a logic that holds the seemingly contradictory ideas of "family values" and "economic individualism" together through the larger framework of the public/private, self/other divide.

The rhetoric of H.B. 2012 makes particularly visible the complexities, conjunctures, and contradictions of neoliberal culture and economics. The bill is not merely a site where immigrants are branded as "others" in order for a nation to deny its economically porous border. Instead, immigrants *are* those "other-others" but they are *also* "others" who must be accepted, protected, and brought into the state's borders in order to reify the cultural and economic status quo. At once, immigrants become both a generalized and a variegated category. They protect the private economies and comfort of white citizens by maintaining their homes, raising their children, and mowing their lawns. Lauren Berlant sees these identifications as central to the neoliberal public sphere. Where "the political sphere is not void of rational thought, its dominant rhetorical style is to recruit the public to see political attachments as an amalgam of reflexive opinion and visceral or 'gut' feeling" ("Epistemology of State Emotion 47). So the immigrants in H.B. 2012 are representations of "rational economic actors" but also "visceral threats" that must be managed. As I will discuss in chapters two and three, they are marked as threats who must be expelled or contained in order to define the sanctity and safety of the American family and American citizenship.

The desire to define an idealized national citizenry against "others" supports a neoliberal logic wherein the image of a coherent, imagined community is used to solidify national borders during a historical moment when U.S. political power and economic opportunity is becoming more and more diffuse due to open trade agreements, offshoring of labor and goods, and global monetary exchange. In the example above, immigrants are defined as both outside the nation, but inside the Texas economy. In a sense, immigrant "others" become both outsiders of the community and insiders of the economy. But they also function rhetorically to allow Texas citizens to define themselves as distinctly American—those who want to protect their economy and borders from immigrant labor and bodies—but also distinctly Texan—those who see their private homes as different and, above all, separate from public governance and the public economy.

The role of the "other" and the "other-other," as Sara Ahmed discusses, are two sides of neoliberal nation building in western countries. "Others" are the people the nation can "save" or show "benevolence" to by allowing them into the economy and culture of the nation, thus allowing the nation to become multicultural. The "other-other" (on the other hand) is the one who cannot be interpolated into culture. He/she must be expelled, sent away, deported in order for the nation to define and imagine itself, its borders, and its citizenry. According to Ahmed, both "others" and "other-others" are central to determining a national identity— much like an imagined community once was[8]—in the wake of neoliberal shifts in economic policy and political exchange. Now, instead of relying solely on common assumptions of economic frameworks, politically inscribed borders, or identities, other bodies—both foreign and domestic— serve as key means to define nationhood.

The phenomenon Ahmed observes is not just a national one. It is a neoliberal cultural one wherein the "other" and/or the "other-other" can be observed at multiple scales—the individual ("it's about my maid, my gardener, and my nanny"), the local, the national, and the international (rogue states, terrorist networks, or even asylum seekers)—to create a sense of community and/or define the borders of the nation-state. But in addition to the mere construction of community, othering also allows for something more insidious. It allows for a masking of the economic and ideological practices which drive neoliberalism at all scales.[9] In fact, we see Ahmed's othering at work in the H.B. 2012 example above. By exempting those members of the immigrant labor force who work for private individuals within the domestic sphere, the legislation creates two sets of immigrants. One set serves our private homes and *should* be included in a limited way, at least according to this law, in the state. Another works for large corporations, presumably taking jobs from those

who might want them, and *must* be expelled from the state. According to
the legislators in support of H.B. 2012, however, the exception is not
about bodies; rather, it is all about economics.[10] The bill is never discussed as a means to protect the borders of the United States. Instead, it is
forwarded as a means to control the economic choices made by citizens of
the state of Texas. The exceptions were merely included in order to specify the most significant economic threats in terms of their use of immigrant labor. The idea that economics drive our legislative and even personal decisions has been tied to the development of neoliberalism.

Wendy Brown, building from Michel Foucault's famous claim that
neoliberal subjects are *homo economicus* by nature (Foucault, "On Governmentality"), asserts that the logics of neoliberalism have penetrated even
our most intimate spheres. "In making the individual fully responsible
for her or himself, neoliberalism equates moral responsibility with rational action; it erases the discrepancy between economic and moral behavior
by configuring morality entirely as a matter of rational deliberation about
costs, benefits, and consequences" (Brown 6). According to Brown, neoliberalism removes the buffer between economics and morals, and
creates a world wherein moral decisions are made through a cost-benefit
analysis of what will affect the self. So in the case of Texas, we see a belief
that immigration law is not about irrational fear of the "other." Instead it
is about rational economic consequences of labor and trade agreements.

But the law is truly about regulating who is an excepted member of
the nation-state and who is not. Furthermore, it establishes the limits of
who will be accepted as a citizen and who will not. So even though
immigrants who work in our homes *must* be the exception because they
do not cause an economic burden, they will never be granted citizenship.
That exception confirms the fact that they are vital to Texas's private
property laws and economic priorities—and these property laws and economic priorities determine how the neoliberal nation-state defines citizens. These are the values that create imagined community in neoliberalism.

The U.S. government's commitment to the needs of private citizens
was supported through the Keynesian welfare state wherein the government provided funding to public institutions that supported the private
growth of its citizens. Furthermore, the governmental support of social
services was underpinned by the ideology that it was part of the government's social contract with its citizens to provide care and support
through institutional structures funded with individual and corporate tax
dollars and provided by government spending. However, this model and
system of belief shifted radically in the 1970s, and continued to erode
during the 1980s under the Reagan administration. Instead of maintaining that it was the government's job to support its citizens, the U.S.
government began to follow the economic philosophy put forth by Milton Friedman and The Chicago School which claimed that successful

governments did not intervene in the "free-market." Once this economic theory was adopted in the United States, the Keynesian welfare state was diminished, and the U.S. government began limiting taxes on both corporations and individuals, thus creating a deficit of funds to provide to large social institutions (Harvey *A Brief History of Neoliberalism*).

Yet as the economic support for social programs waned, so did the government's commitment to the liberal social contract. Instead, through the rhetoric of personal responsibility the government tied care of private citizens to the private realm. According to Lisa Duggan, it is the deep connection between privatization in economics and personal responsibility that marks the change from Keynesian to neoliberal economics. She states, "The valorized concepts of *privatization* and *personal responsibility* travel widely across the rhetorics of contemporary policy debates, joining economic goals with cultural values while obscuring the identity politics and upwardly redistributive impetus of neoliberalism" (Duggan 14).

Duggan's focus on the yoking of cultural and economic forces is critical for the work of this book. Much as Brown articulates a historical conjunction between economic liberalism and neoconservative ideology as the defining characteristic of neoliberal thought, Duggan is defining U.S. neoliberalism through the rhetoric of *privatization*—the move to place economic responsibility on the individual corporation or citizen— and *personal responsibility*—the move to make individuals responsible for their own private welfare and social conditions. Ong also sees these connections clearly articulated throughout the presidencies of Ronald Reagan and George H.W. Bush. Instead of committing to a social contract, Reagan and Bush both advocated "personal responsibility" as a means of recognizing oneself as a U.S. citizen. "Bush calls his new vision the 'ownership society,' an explicit claim that American citizenship under his watch will shift toward a primitive, narrow vision of citizenship that includes only property owners, privileging 'an independent and egotistical individual' in isolated pursuit of economic self-interest" (Ong 2). For Ong, the linking of economics to social programs has major ramifications for citizenship and the national imaginary. U.S. citizens, in particular, are asked to see themselves as citizens not because of their national affiliation, but rather because of their commitment to the pursuit of economic self-interest.

As I have demonstrated, it is not only the Texas legislature's commitment to exception in the name of private economic interest, but also it is defining of "types" of acceptable and non-acceptable immigrants that demonstrates how a cost-benefit analysis alone does not drive the decisions of legislators and voters. The forwarding of immigrant bodies, instead of creating a discussion about economic or immigrant policy, reveals the mystifying capacity of the neoliberal exception. In this case, as with the examples discussed throughout the book, branding serves as the rhetorical means by which this mystification is forwarded. By branding immigrants in the legislation, the discussions surrounding H.B. 2012 remain limited to the exception, not the complex connections between immigration policy, economic policy, and nationalist ideology that are at play. However, when critically analyzed, H.B. 2012 reveals the complex webs of power, economic, and affective exchange that are central to questions of immigration. These questions suggest a process of affect and identification that draws on individuals' anxieties and desires as well as their self-definitions as economic citizens. These are classed citizens—people who see themselves as middle class because of economic citizenship. The immigrants called forth within the bill are not seen in the same way as the citizens to whom the bill offers protection. Instead, they are evacuated of subjectivity and forwarded as "terms" or economic features, not subjects, bodies, or people.

The move to *use* bodies and/or subjects and commodities within capitalism marks a shift away from liberal governmentality, and it is represented through the practice of branding seen in the legislation above. The immigrants in H.B. 2012, regardless of the type of "other" they represent, are not forwarded as people who need compassion. Instead they are put forth as economic factors and/or threats to or supporters of the U.S. status quo. In other words, their exceptional status is not about immigration or the immigrants at all; it is about U.S. neoliberal citizens. The focus, then, is placed on the way brands are used to create specific narratives of those others and other-others: what they have done, what they may do, what they may not do, who they can or cannot be. If there is ever discussion of the economic conditions which engender these brands, they are discussed in relation to the branding of bodies who are then forwarded as exceptions to or reasons for the conditions at hand.

As a counter to Brown's theory of cost-benefit ethics and values clarification, I offer a somewhat different view of neoliberal political engagement. I argue that the U.S. public identifies and makes choices surrounding their daily lives not only by rational responses to circumstance or by the influence of political address but also through the influence of *affect*. Their affective responses, and how they are stimulated within neoliberal conditions, are complex and are not represented by strict emotional stimuli and responses to political speeches and/or platforms. Instead, those responses are organized around material and economic structures, which then create affective responses.

According to Wendy Hesford, *affective identification* is created in the cultural context in which the rhetor is speaking or writing. Instead of looking at identification as a means to find similar traits and identities, Hesford argues that we must attend to the embedded and seemingly commonplace "cues" that help us to navigate and communicate in a particular context ("Kairos and the Geopolitical Rhetorics"). These "cues" are not always created through logical recognition, but instead are often affective responses based in affinities which are created through intangible or unintelligible contexts such as memory, emotion, and preference. It is within these realms that neoliberal rhetoric and the technology of branding operate. Identification is still central to this practice,[11] but it is through the identification with and against particular groups that this process begins to "move" people emotionally.

Affective identification uses language and images to create responses which are often extralinguistic—visceral or somatic. Affective identification works as a backdrop of feeling that resonates with histories, rhetorics, and images that are not evoked directly, but that circulate to connect our memories and bodies. These histories are not necessarily stated directly, but circulate through the brand, much as "[n]eoliberalism organizes material and political life *in terms of* race, gender, and sexuality as well as economic class and nationality, or ethnicity and religion" (Duggan 3). Because of these schema of organization, neoliberal subjects come to know the world through their identification (or non-identification) with those specific categories. Branding, then, works as a means to circulate these identities relying on the fact these histories and identities are ingrained into our memories and understandings of our current cultural moment. Therefore, it is not about explicitly arguing the criminal status of immigrants, but rather it is about creating a law with an exception that is not questioned, because it is demonstrative of current neoliberal technologies and logics.

FROM OTHER-OTHERS TO BRANDS: COMMODIFYING BODIES

Within our current geopolitical context, the economic anxieties created by neoliberal globalization, the U.S. government, media (both mainstream and independent sources), and grassroots organizations (cast as both liberal and conservative), have used both gay/lesbian/bisexual/transgendered (GLBT) bodies and immigrant bodies as *others* to define the borders of the nation-state and to shore up *homo economicus*. They have done this through the branding of those bodies, by evacuating them of meaning and circulating their images as representative of otherness and exception. Much like the branding we see in advertising, branding of others creates an association with a "lifestyle" and corporate agenda, or in this case the agenda of the nation-state, rather than the item or body itself. Through this rhetorical action, as I will explain later in this chapter and develop in chapter two, even people who are stripped of human characteristics and the protections of the neoliberal nation-state are placed in the service of neoliberal capital.

These branded bodies serve capital both as underclassed labor, but also as brands who stimulate the emotions and desires of the U.S. citizenry. The brands put forward have "affective economies" unto themselves that are not stable. The notion of an *affective economy* is a site wherein feelings circulate creating the conditions for emotional identification, response or action. According to Ahmed, "emotions work as a form of capital: affect does not reside positively in the sign or commodity, but is produced only as an effect of its circulation" ("Affective Economies" 120). Her discussion of the economics of emotion is not merely a psychoanalytic conception of emotion, wherein the circulation of emotions is charted. Ahmed's work is an attempt to place Marxist markers of surplus value onto those ideas of circulation as well. The context, mode of circulation, and intensity of the reaction are all key factors in understanding how affect moves and gains value. For Ahmed, and as I will explain later in terms of branding and rhetoric, emotions are economic in that they gain value through their circulation. Brands gain two types of value: economic and identificatory value.

These are not mutually exclusive values, but emotions (for Ahmed) and brands (for me) work both as commodities and the meanings that make commodities intelligible. Rachel Riedner suggests, "When we talk about value we're talking about things that are meaningful (i.e., I value this object because it embodies a value I identify with . . .) but we're also talking about how things that are meaningful are attached to capitalist production, how circulation of objects (such as news stories) enables exchange, produces surplus for capital, and how objects reproduce cultural systems and affective identifications of value" (*Responsibility at a Distance* 15). Brands work to commodify bodies and allow them to circulate, thus assisting in the production of surplus value and bolstering the U.S. economy through the mystification of the laboring bodies that they brand. But they are also valuable to neoliberal subjects who need to identify particular images and values as American. As I will discuss later in this chapter, brands serve to give the U.S. public meaningful sites of identification in a time of anxiety and inequality.

In that sense, brands and emotions are highly contextual and dependent on exchange. They do not have inherent value in themselves or when housed within a body. Rhetoric and branding, like emotions, gain surplus value through their specific cultural exchanges. As such, certain emotions/brands/rhetoric(s) build in value, some decrease in value, and others remain constant. Emotions can change their value depending upon the context of exchange. For example, news of H.B. 2012 did not circulate within the state of Texas. Instead, the U.S. media and other state media outlets found the exception to the law newsworthy. But within the state of Texas, most citizens and lawmakers found the law *intelligible* and above all *reasonable*. The reaction of Texans to the law is due in large part to their comfort with privatization and the centrality of private interest within the state's legislative framework. In other states within the United States, California for example, that do not commit as strongly to the rhetoric of private interest (even if economically they follow many of the privatizing features of it), H.B. 2012 seemed like an affront to immigration legislation. The presence of the private labor exception made explicit the unspoken inequalities surrounding immigration. Whether the exception sparked discomfort for liberals in California who claim to stand for "fair immigration reform" (a more complete discussion of California's immigration legislation is present in chapter two), or for those in Alabama or Arizona who see immigration as exception-less, H.B. 2012 carried much more affective value as its rhetoric circulated outside of Texas.

Ahmed's notion of affect as economic allows us to understand that not only do emotions circulate, but they carry differential economic and affective value depending where, when, and how they travel. As emotions circulate, they collect value, but they also produce surplus value because there cannot be a one-to-one correspondence between the emotion and the referent. Instead, emotions move through circuits of exchange gaining and losing value (or intensity) depending on a variety of factors present within the exchange. It is not a mere event and subsequent response that creates the value within circulation, but instead, it is the abstraction and exchange of the emotion as it moves between people, places, and objects that allows for the development of surplus value.

Therefore, Ahmed's reading of affective economies is not another move to capitalize emotions—much as Foucault's *homo economicus*. She does not attempt to create another more complex version of a rational neoliberal economic subject. Her focus on emotions disrupts that narrative, much as my reading of Texas's H.B. 2012 challenged Brown's claim to neoliberal rationality. Instead, what Ahmed is arguing for is a recognition that capitalist structures have infiltrated our most intimate understandings of the world but *not* by making us into rational actors. Instead it is by making us *reactive*, in the sense that we make decisions based on ideological and economic "cues" (to use Hesford's term). As these cues circulate, they do not follow an inherent logic. Instead, it is through their movement and the *processes* of circulation, exchange, and accumulation that meaning is created and understood.

Branding circulates much like emotion because, as I have discussed, it creates both economic and identificatory value. As a practice, it developed as a corporate marketing strategy designed to connect consumers with products not by extolling the uses of that product, but instead, by selling what that product can *mean* to a consumer's life. "The purpose of brand management is to guide the investments of affect on the part of consumers (or other subjects). . . . It is a matter of creating an affective intensity, an experience of unity between the brand and the subject" (Arvidsson 93). Adam Arvidsson's definition of brand management echoes Ahmed's discussion of affect. It is not how the brand is defined, but it is the interaction between the brand and the subject that creates value in the process of branding. In other words, Nike and its representational "swoosh" is not a successful brand because of the swoosh logo. Instead, it is successful because of how that swoosh translates into an emotional identification for consumers. Consumers do not purchase Nike because of the swoosh, but rather they recognize the swoosh to represent all the meanings and investments they hope to gain from interaction with the products which possess it—athleticism, endurance, and strength.

As a marketing strategy, then, branding focuses on affective value. It is about connecting the symbols attached to products to consumers in an emotional way. In its purest form, it can be seen as a semiotic endeavor wherein the sign of the product is given meaning through the affective exchange with the consumer. In other words, brands do not project their meaning or value onto consumers; it is a consistent contextual exchange that allows them to be successful in the marketplace (Lury *Brands*). Once again, this could be seen in the ways immigrants were branded in the discussion of H.B. 2012. The meanings assigned to immigrant labor were only emotionally valuable when they circulated outside Texas state lines. Within the state, it was a given that these "brand" identities were central to the economic value of immigrant labor within Texas.

Branding, as a facet of advertising, is not about product placement or the product at all; rather it is about developing an identity or "lifestyle" into which groups of products then fit. In this sense, it can be understood how easily it could be shifted to realms outside of what can be seen as purely economic exchange. As branding developed over the course of the twentieth century and global corporate power continues to be the reigning political and economic logic of our time, branding will continue to grow until people's lives will be so completely dictated by this consumerist model that they can "move right into their lifestyle choice" and watch their consumption habits become their reality (Klein *No Logo*). Much like the identities and jobs of the domestic workers in H.B. 2012, the products are *almost* insignificant in this exchange or the products are secondary to their affective identification, but instead their representational (or surplus) value is what becomes meaningful. If the value of the product is not considered, the labor of the product is completely invisible. Branding, then, is the ultimate production of a hyper-capitalist society.

When bodies are branded, people become no more than cogs in corporate or political machines, just like objects.[12] No longer do bodies carry material identities nor do they carry the potential for citizenship—they're not immigrants following the American dream who can eventually be incorporated into national identity, like Ahmed's others and other-others. Instead, branded bodies become void of any individuizing markers. Much like the H.B. 2012 example, the immigrant bodies did not carry subjectivities. Instead they were merely "houseworkers" or "corporate employees." They were merely brands representing particular economic categories that served a common vision of a Texas lifestyle. They were the representations of corporate interests. Individuals become data sets to be given over to authorities, corporations, medical services, and so on. It is through the monitoring of those statistics that the state and other powerful entities (private security companies, insurance carriers, corporations) monitor and allow individuals to act.

In the shift away from a disciplinary society,[13] it is not the internalization of discipline that is of primary importance. Instead, it is economic and market driven data that is important and controls who can and cannot participate in society. As I have discussed, through the logic of exception, a permanent underclass is developed, one that will never have access to citizenship. This is great for capitalism because it is no longer regulated by the legalities of the liberal nation-state. Instead, it is regulated through numbers, quotas, and other abstract measures of quantification,[14] thus leaving the actual bodies and identities and the nation-state's responsibility to them out of the discussion completely.

This is further supported by the transition to a society of control wherein even citizens are regulated by numbers and quantifiable indicators. For example, a credit score is of far more value than moral character or criminal behavior because it determines a citizen's ability to enter into capitalism. Therefore, credit scores are not only determining individuals' abilities to purchase commodities, but they are now also used in the hiring process for certain jobs.[15] For Deleuze, the society of control, one where corporate culture and commitments have distorted our most basic disciplinary structures, is above all a society of monitoring (*not* surveillance in the Foucauldian sense) wherein people become the fragmentation of their data and their parts. In other words, people are their credit scores, medical history, and social security numbers. They are not human beings, disciplined or not. "Individuals have become '*dividuals*,' and masses, samples, data, markets, or '*banks*.' Perhaps it is money that expresses the distinction between the two societies best, since discipline always referred back to minted money that locks gold as numerical standard, while control relates to floating rates of exchange, modulated according to a rate established by a set of standard currencies" ("Postscript on the Societies of Control" 5).

Deleuze uses the example of currency, which in the classical Marxist sense is the beginning of surplus value, to demonstrate the shift away from discipline, in which there is a concrete correspondence—money to gold. Money, in economic terms, supposedly has a one to one correspondence with gold. However, as Marx describes in *Capital vol. 1*, that correspondence is not as concrete as one might think because it mystifies the products' relationship to labor through its exchange for money[16]—which is often not earned through labor in the bourgeois class.

However in a society of control, those concrete correspondences become purely representational. Deleuze argues that the connecting of money to exchange rates or corporate externalities demonstrates a different representational relationship than money to gold. Exchange rates and corporate externalities are never fixed or tied directly to specific sums of money. They can always be shifted by the influences of the market, politicians, or the economy at large. Therefore, the correspondence between money and exchange rates is not based on a relationship between fixed identities. Instead it is based on a relationship between representations that are constantly in flux.

Within this context, it is not difficult to understand how in the media and political arena images and descriptions of individuals, as well as statistics and data about certain groups, can become brands. No longer is the immigrant, the worker, the GLBT person a subject or potential citizen. He/she is an image, a sound bite, or a meme to be forwarded in the name of a particular political platform. Once branded, these bodies are rhetorical constructions that are used in the name of governmentality or to gain purchase in the market or the political arena. Either way, the material contexts and conditions of these bodies—their histories, their complex relationships to the economy and ideology—are evacuated and their identities become much the same as a credit score, a mere identifying factor that can be used in the name of capital. Through branding the complexities of economics, politics, and history are removed and replaced with the promise of an attractive lifestyle that can be attainable by a simple exchange.

AFFECTIVE BRANDING: BODIES DISSOLVE INTO THE NATION-STATE

One might wonder, since branding is such a pernicious practice, why has it translated so easily into the political realm? As I show in chapter two through my discussion of the branding of the term family, branding creates an evacuated representation of one group of bodies. But it does so in order to create a coherent and even seamless vision of another community of bodies. Much like Ahmed's othering, branding allows for the development of a communal or national identity in a time when such an identity seems fragmented and diffuse. So yes, branding does remove bodies and creates images detached from concrete productions of humanity (much like branding in advertising removes the product, and thus the labor required to make said product, from the selling of the corporate image). But there is something affective and persuasive in the mobilization of branding. It works because it makes people who see themselves as citizens "feel" better, less confused, more at home in the world.

To take this back to the H.B. 2012 example, the Texas legislature can "feel better" by mobilizing an immigration law that penalizes some immigrants that are "other-other" and thus too foreign to be included in the state (or we can extrapolate the nation-state). But still included are those who are only "other," those who can be included and brought into the borders of the nation-state as comprehensible foreigners who we can help. Thus we feel magnanimous about our willingness to make this exception.

Ghassan Hage describes this phenomenon with respect to Australia. He discusses how the Australian public can provide the "gift of citizenship" to particular groups of immigrants whom they believe can add to the multicultural image of Australia. However, those who do not add to that image are expelled, banned, and not granted any path to asylum or citizenship.[17] By providing certain "others" the right to become Australian citizens, the national body is defining a mythic "whole Australia nationality" that can include or reject particular groups who can or cannot "fit in" (*White Nation*). Additionally, Hage argues, by granting some immigrants rights to citizenship it gives the national body the "feeling" that they are a benevolent, multicultural, and progressive country.

This "feeling of benevolence" and the creating of a "mythic Australian unified nationality" is of particular interest to Hage. As he sees it, by granting some and not others citizenship and creating a multicultural nation-state, Australia is reaffirming the myth of the "white nation" that is full of those who are kind and willing to grant those who are not white "the gift of becoming citizens" or "like whites." Through this process, there is a distancing of the very complex legal, cultural, and economic realities that buttress Australia's national history and current immigration debates. For example, Australia has a rich and complex history of settlement that includes indigenous peoples, as well as immigrants. However, most of the indigenous tribes have been pushed into the bush and have fought for land rights, much like the Native Americans in the United States. Furthermore, the initial settlers of Australia were not solely white. Since its inception as Britain's penal colony, Australia has struggled with the legacy of raced bodies on the continent. Therefore, Australia's past is one checkered with racial and classed struggles, which the narrative of a "white nation" purposely occludes. What said narrative provides instead is a soothing narrative of "wholeness" and "benevolence" that is both simplistic and easily identifiable, even if it is not readily recognizable.

This same desire for national "wholeness" and "simplicity" can be seen in current political discourse across the United States. For example, Thomas Frank's book *What's the Matter With Kansas?*, asks how one of the poorest Midwestern states can continually vote for and produce legislation that seems to defy the basic needs and best interests of its citizens. His argument, ultimately, is that the people in Kansas are not voting their own interests, but instead are voting for an image of an America that no longer and has never really existed. This is one in which white, middle class, Christian people are both statistically and politically central to the progress and continued success of the United States. Frank does an excellent job articulating how the Republican party (Grand Old Party, or GOP) has mobilized the image of a coherent national identity at the expense of workers, immigrants, and even GLBT people. By creating a narrative of "family values" and "protecting the nation," the GOP has solidified a powerful brand-image of an America wherein foreigners and other-others must either be "converted" or expelled.

The persuasive power of this brand, according to Frank, is that it allows the very workers it attacks to see themselves as part of the brand—not outside of it—because it provides enough difference from others that fall outside of the brand that one can easily place oneself inside of it. For example, according to Frank the average resident of Kansas has been laid-off from factory or blue-collar work and has to find employment in the service sector. This is a direct result of the offshoring of manufacturing following the passage of the GOP (and Democratic) supported North American Free Trade Agreement (NAFTA) and the Central American Free Trade Agreement (CAFTA) during the 1990s. These shifts in employment have affected the average income, ability to access health insurance, and the daily lives of Kansans. Yet, instead of voting for or attempting to influence change that would materially better their way of life, Kansas's voters continually vote for GOP candidates who continue to support and implement further outsourcing, off-shoring, and corporate tax breaks.

When Frank inquired as to why the Kansans voted how they did, overwhelmingly, they did not cite these economic platforms, but instead would cite candidates' position statements on "family values issues," such as abortion or gay marriage and "immigration" issues that were not even on the Kansas ballot (*What's the Matter with Kansas?*). Frank's claim is that the results of the elections in Kansas reveal that American voters no longer want to engage with issues. Instead, voters are seduced by the ideology and branding that permeates politics today. However, I suggest that Frank's book reveals how branding in the political arena can serve to seemingly "simplify" and thus "soothe" the public during a time when politics and daily life are becoming both complex and destabilized. By focusing the discussion on brands, citizens do not have to understand the complexities of their job loss and political disenfranchisement. Instead, they can focus their political concerns on the brands of immigrants or other bodies who are not seen as acceptable. The branding of others, then serves to help Kansans feel more secure in a time of economic insecurity.

But perhaps a better word to describe the lives of those in Kansas is unequal rather than unstable. Their lives may feel unstable, without the security of a well paying job, a clear sense of their place within a larger national picture, and a constant struggle to keep their family healthy and fulfilled without consistent access to health insurance. However, these are the effects of the inequality that drives neoliberal capitalism. Without it, neoliberal capitalism would return to earlier incarnations of capital wherein the factory was king, production and labor were necessary parts of the accumulation process, and profits were not created in such vast excess that only the top one percent of the United States held a vast disproportionate amount of the wealth of the country. As Jodi Dean states: "[Neoliberalism] makes a few winners—top 1 percent—and a lot of losers. *[N]eoliberal competition is select (partial), brutal, and for the benefit of the top one percent."* (emphasis in original Dean, Roundtable).

So branding not only makes those who are not part of that top one percent "feel better." It also makes them feel a part of the very system that is using them to insure that a select few remain rich. It does so by exploiting the anxieties of those who are not in the top one percent. In order to quell those anxieties it offers a vision of America wherein they are still valued members of society—a citizenry with meaningful histories and values to which they can attach. It is the use of others and the branding of those bodies in the name of family values that is at the heart of neoliberal governmentality today in order to mask the blatant economic inequalities at work.

Branding, then, serves to create a narrative of America, much like the one Hage presented of Australia, wherein the U.S. national identity is seamless, whole, and unified. This of course is a myth, and is another extrapolation of Benedict Anderson's idea of an imagined community whereby newspapers, television, and shared events allowed nations to construct their collective identity. Much as I have argued that H.B. 2012 mediates a Texan identity both in need of immigration reform, and private property security, Anderson demonstrates that Europe's seemingly core supranational identity is constructed across vast material and ideological differences through mediated images, which are imbued with meaning through a collective agreement that the representation of events are/were important and should be understood in the same way, even though there may be a variety of interpretations possible. For Anderson, imagined communities work to mask the material differences in service of a greater national identity. For imagined communities to work, there must be some acknowledgement that even though there *are* differences, the similarities that come with national identity can overcome those differences in the name of nationhood and shared identity.

This is where branding and imagined communities differ. Branding, unlike an imagined community, does not admit or assume difference because it does not have to. Remember production, labor, and the actual products (or bodies in this case) are inconsequential in branding. Instead, branding seeks to create the image of a coherent national identity that disregards difference and material circumstances altogether. Instead, what it offers is almost a mirage—the hope for an uncomplicated future where difference and complexity is expelled or made invisible through exception or the yearning for a history of that same "white nation" where difference never existed in the first place. Now both of these offerings eschew the obvious schisms within politics, democracy, economics, and ultimately reality. But reality is not the point of branding; representation is. This is because reality must be accounted for and representation can be consumed.

But the consumption of brands is not always employed for positive associations. In fact, some of the most powerful brands at work in the political arena are ones meant to instill those very anxieties which brands such as "family," "family values," and "white nation" seek to ameliorate. An example of the collusion between anxiety and amelioration in the name of political gain was discussed in *The Shock Doctrine: The Rise of Disaster Capitalism*. Naomi Klein claims that the key characteristic of the shift to free market, laissez-faire corporatist economics is that of shock.[18] According to Klein, Milton Freidman's claim is that if nations took advantage of the state of shock surrounding disasters and catastrophic events, they would more readily pass through legislation to end the Keynesian welfare state once and for all.

Klein's articulation of the consequences of shock is not only descriptive of the economic and political exigency of shock. Instead, she also claims that one of the most important characteristics of shock is the way it makes people *feel*, and it is from that space of *feeling* that people are persuaded to act. It is not merely rational or persuasive rhetoric that prompts change or apathy in the body politic, but rather it is through a rhetorically and materially produced state of *feeling*—fear, confusion, anger, disassociation—that the body politic is prompted to seek solace in the government's rhetoric and policies.[19]

The feelings of fear and anxiety created through these shocks can shake an individual's sense of identity to the core. Without strong governmental social services upon which to fall back, citizens are left searching for a way to ground their identities—both individual and national. As I have argued earlier in this chapter, the two are often intertwined. Jodi Dean, in her book *Neoliberal Fantasies*, looks at the complexities of neoliberal capital in the context of identity formation. Building from Slavoj Žižek's theory of the decline of symbolic efficiency,[20] she argues that due to the decline of the welfare state, state run disciplinary venues no longer hold the power over individuals that they once did. Instead, individuals now have a much more fluid sense of identity, which according to Dean, leads to great anxiety and fear among the general population. She writes: "The fluidity and adaptability of imaginary identities is accompanied by a certain fragility and insecurity. Imaginary identities are incapable of establishing a firm place to stand, a position from which one can make sense of one's world" (Dean 67). Although this may seem as if the lack of pre-determined or normative identities would provide a certain space for individual "play" (to use Derrida's term) with identity, Dean demonstrates that without a clear means of identification, most neoliberal subjects are left searching for stable ways with which to define themselves.

Instead of being freer to develop individual and shifting identities that produce more possibilities, and as Žižek might say *jouissance*, the lack of established ideological models and disciplinary input creates anxiety and a process of individuation that is incomplete, and thus always searching for a new more stable identity. Therefore, Dean argues, it is not unrealistic that people do not hold to political positions (or ideological ones for that matter) in the ways one might expect. Instead, individuals are often swayed by that which can provide comfort, stability, and group affiliation. That is what seems to provide individual satisfaction.

It is not that individuals do not have the possibility of forming identities outside of this process. Rather, it is that the identities that are possible become increasingly limited due to the political and social realities of neoliberalism. Prior to the development of hyper-capitalism in the early 1970s, Louis Althusser argued that individuals relied on ideological state apparatuses (ISAs) to develop their identities. ISAs were a product of a disciplinary society and were supported by forms of governmentality that privileged biopower and the factory. It was all about discipline. However, as discussed earlier in this chapter, we are no longer in a disciplinary society. Instead, we are now in a society of control. Therefore, the ways in which individuals develop identities in relationship to the state (or the corporation) has changed.

Instead of becoming disciplined through schools, churches, factories, or the government, individuals are now facing a historic moment where their identities are tied to discrete sets of fragmented information—they are *dividuals*, after all. Therefore, it becomes more and more difficult to create a coherent and stable identity in relation to the state. Not only has what is valued of their identities changed, but also the role of the state in determining those values has changed dramatically. These changes in both the value of individual information and identities and also state governmentality structures create the anxiety to which Dean is referring.

Dean's claims regarding individual anxiety and its connection to the social and economic conditions produced by neoliberalism are compelling when put in the context of shock outlined by Klein. Furthermore, it creates fertile ground for branding to influence whole swaths of the population. If branding is indeed both simplifying of humanity and affecting of it at the same time, the psychological needs of neoliberal subjects make them ideal candidates to be affected by branding. Because "the flip side of the multiplicity of imaginary identities, then, is a reduction and congealing of identity into massive sites or strange attractors of affective investment" (Dean 67). Instead of being coherent, identity becomes a series of emotional responses to what is affectively attractive to the individual. If a desire for stability and the escape from anxiety is key to a neoliberal subject's identity, creating a brand that presents a nation that is stable, comfortable, and safe will create affective identification.

Branding offers just this kind of succor in a time of subjective anxiety. "Like commercial brands, the political brand is an answer to the home-lessness of post-modern subjects. . . . This identification is generally framed, not in terms of rational interest, but in terms of emotional experi-ences" (Arvidsson 92–93). Part of what the connection to varied sources, and the response to a multiplicity of attractors reveals about branding and the formation of identity in neoliberalism is that both are necessarily fragmentary and conjunctural. Although at any given moment, branding seems to present a seamless and non-complicated image of a whole, it really can be a shifting representation of an item or body evacuated of its material value. Brands can also conjoin in order to shift representations between one another and build a more comprehensive view of threat, comfort, or whatever kind of lifestyle they are trying to portray. When placed together brands become much like the identities Dean discusses above. They become an assemblage.

RHETORICAL ASSEMBLAGE: THE *WORK* OF BRANDING BODIES

Whether it is presented through branding, or it is created in response to affective investments, an assemblage—the fragmentary, shifting, and representative nature of identity—works by presenting identities of bod-ies together as co-determinates or contiguous identifiers. These are not causal relationships, but instead they are fluid, in motion, always shift-ing. Jasbir Puar argues that rhetoric is not only used to produce inten-sities or feelings, but it creates an assemblage of "othering" that requires totalizing governmental and occasionally coercive means of protection. She draws upon post–9/11 rhetorics of terror to demonstrate how "other-others" are mobilized by amalgamating features and histories so as to create "assembled" threats. Puar defines the assemblage as "a series of dispersed but mutually implicated networks, drawn together by enuncia-tion and dissolution, causality and effect" ("Queer Times" 127). Much like Cecilia Lury's description of consumer brand combinations as semi-otic, Puar describes how identificatory assemblages work to join together a network of characteristics which can then be transferred between bod-ies through the process of branding to create particular affective values.

I will examine the theoretical literature of assemblage in more depth in chapter three, but to understand how brands are assembled to produce intense threats, I now look to the work of Brian Massumi. He focuses on the production of "threats" to show how fear becomes removed from its initial event referent, is combined with other memories of fear, and then *reassembled* into new events with an increased magnitude of fear that is not directly proportional or even applicable to the event at hand.[21] The reactions and associations created, because of this imperceptible joining of discrete events of fear, are central to the development and deployment of the rhetoric of neoliberalism. It is the deployment of threat to incite fear that Massumi sees as a critical feature in the rhetoric of neoliberal geopolitics. Because threats are often multifarious, insidious, and non-containable, they become even more threatening when they are amalgamations of combined (if not disassociated) referents.

The assemblage, then, can be a quite powerful means of creating affective value in our current times of sound bites, terror alerts, and buzz-words. Instead of having meaningful exchanges wherein references must be explained and connections coherently mapped through content, the assemblage allows for any referents to become meaningful just through the nature of their placement in a meme, news story, or piece of legislation. According to Manuel DeLanda, we assemble meaning by placing words, phrases, and in the case of this study—brands—contiguously. They then become *territorialized* and *coded* or *decoded*, or as Rebecca Dingo would say *networked*,[22] throughout their exchange. An assemblage is never complete, nor is it stable. It is always changing due to its context.

Assembling brands, much like affect, only gains meaning and value through exchange. That exchange, however, is by no means performed in a vacuum. In fact, much of the value created in both consumer and political branding relies on historical narratives about identities and human characteristics in order for the brands to become affectively valuable. According to Puar, identities, and I would argue brands, are both palimp-sestic and scrambled,[23] which leads to a critique of the ways in which language represents brands, bodies, and histories as discrete and individual. Instead of focusing on products or persons with centered or fixed identities, the process of branding creates identities through affective exchange (to return to Ahmed). This leads to seemingly stable identities that are *valuable* objects, but, as Riedner discussed, do not contain complex subjectivities. Instead, brands are used to forward an image of a possible subjecthood that is simply defined, and thus compelling during a time of neoliberal economic and political flux.

Brands, then, stir emotions and appease the public not at the rational level that rhetorical practice often claims.[24] But branding engages emotions in a way that seems logical, and it does this because it speaks to the U.S. public on visceral levels. According to Massumi, affect can be seen as pre-emotion, thus almost pre-rational. Affect, when seen as such, is often discussed as intensity. Words, brands, body language effect us with an intensity that is not rational because it speaks to embedded memories and cultural understandings. These intensities work to create circumstances in which identifications can happen without language or explicit communication. Intensity is a condition under which events and situations of identification can occur. Jenny Edbauer discusses how intensity is deeply connected to affect through her discussion of President Bush's "folksy affect" and "dottering speech patterns" ("Executive Overspill" 6). Edbauer argues that it does not matter that the President misspeaks, stumbles, squints, or fumbles over words because these tics work at a different register of identification than the words of his speeches. "The event of image reception takes place on several levels: there is a level of intensity and a level of qualification. Whereas qualification is the image's 'indexing to conventional meanings in an intersubjective context, its soci-olinguistic qualification,' an image's intensity is 'the strength or duration of the image's effect' (Massumi 24)" ("Executive Overspill" 8). Not only does the President's speech provide a level of qualification—the meanings of the language determined through word choice and context. It also has a level of intensity that operates at a different register than the language of the speech. The level of intensity operates long after the speech is over, and these recognitions—a visceral, bodily response—can take place out of context, at a later date, or whenever a resonance of intensity is felt.

Although intensities are "virtual," to use Delueze and Massumi's terms, they can still produce "actual" events or materials because of their ability to create relationships between different concepts or entities.[25] Edbauer discusses intensities in terms of "relationality," and it is through relationality that Bush's affective presence creates meaning for the American public. "The feelings that we once attributed to our *selves* are thus reattributed to the affective event of involvement and its sensation. The sociality of affect is precisely this relation among bodies" (14). Instead of creating an event or identification through his language, he has already created one that circulates and helps determine his affective identification prior to his first word. Affective intensities create relationships between bodies before rhetorical situations and events present themselves, and without these visceral and virtual happenings, affective identification would not be as effective.

By drawing on historical narratives about who is a threat, whose bodies are marked, and who can enter into the nation, brands call upon visceral responses that in turn enable their success. As I will discuss in chapter two, the brand of the immigrant as a "bandit" would not be as successful had there not been cultural images of "the Frito Bandito" or fears of new waves of immigrants "stealing" the culture of already-established U.S. citizens. Although these images and narratives no longer dominate the terms of discussion, they maintain cultural relevance due to our historical understandings of and cultural fears associated with immigration. These past images and rhetoric(s) influence the success of the branding of the immigrant today. Therefore, when bodies are branded and assembled there are two levels of meaningful exchange at work. The first is the circulation of the current brand which speaks to the neoliberal anxieties outlined throughout this chapter. The second is the imprint or palimpsestic markings of historical images and narratives upon which the brands are built.

Additionally, as I will discuss in chapter three, current brands can be assembled to create an amorphous threat—the terrorist, enemy combatant, or predator—by placing brands in conjunction with one another. In other words, when the brand of the immigrant bandit is placed in conjunction with the GLBT deviant, an über-brand of predator is formed. This brand is contingent, shifting, and completely contextual, and it is incredibly powerful. Its power lies in its ability to draw upon the features of both brands, yet not have a clear symbolic referent. The terrorist, as I will discuss in chapter three, is an all-encompassing threat that is everywhere and nowhere all at once (Puar and Rai), and the über-brand functions in much the same way. Yet even though it cannot be readily identified, the terrorist is crafted as the most dangerous threat to the nation, and therefore, it is intensely affective.

Thus branding draws on identification, intensity, and affect to move U.S. citizens and give them objects with which to identify or dis/identify when forming both individual and national identities. Furthermore, it enables the mystification of the material labor of the branded bodies, thus supporting the neoliberal economic systems presently in place. In both instances, branding leaves bodies as objects of capital—producing surplus value both economically and emotionally. The rest of the book, as discussed briefly above, will examine specific cases where branding offers a national identity at the cost of the humanity of those it brands. Ultimately, this book will explore how branding, as a technology of neoliberal governmentality, offers some a clear image of citizenship on the bodies of others.

NOTES

1. The penalties proposed are up to a $10,000 fine and/or two years in state prison.

2. The appearance of the terms "exemption" and "exception" is notable. Both Giorgio Agamben and Jasbir Puar discuss current forms of state sovereignty based in the development of exceptions—who is recognized as a citizen, who must be expelled or imprisoned. Within this short news story, it appears the Representatives within the state of Texas see threats to the economy and citizenry of Texas defined by exception as well.

3. Arizona Senate Bill (S.B.) 1070, *The Support Our Law Enforcement and Safe Neighborhoods Act* calls for any immigrant in the United States for over thirty days to register with the state to receive documentation. Subsequently, any immigrant found within Arizona without documentation can be arrested for a misdemeanor. Furthermore, it requires that state and local police to check immigrant status "during lawful stop, detention, or arrest." Finally, harsh penalties for businesses who knowingly hire and employ undocumented workers were also written into the law. It was signed into law on April 23, 2010, and the U.S. Supreme Court upheld its validity in 2012.

4. Robert Mcruer critiques the economics of discourses of inclusion in his book *Crip Theory*. To him, inclusion of difference—bodies, sexualities, gender norms—often is commodified in the name of capital. Therefore, it is not a "true" inclusion, but rather one that serves to reaffirm the dominant heteronormative-ablist culture through notions of acceptance and inclusion.

5. Alabama's House Bill (H.B.) 56, *The Hammon-Beason Alabama Taxpayer and Citizen Protection Act*, is the most stringent anti-immigration legislation in the United States to date. It included a provision that required police to check immigration status upon "reasonable suspicion." It prohibits non-documented immigrants from receiving any public services (welfare, medical care, schooling). It prohibits non-documented immigrants from leasing or purchasing homes and applying for jobs. Finally, it criminalizes the making of false identification, renders contractual agreements between non-documented immigrants and others null and void, and requires proof of citizenship to vote. As of November 23, 2011, the portions of the bill that prohibited the acceptance of public services and seeking housing and employment have been blocked. The rest of the bill, however, stands.

6. There is an assumption here about the feminization of domestic labor, which I will discuss at length in chapter two. Not only are the domestic laborers seen as "non-resistant" because they work in the home, but the job space of the home has been coded as a feminized space for centuries (see Maria Mies). As such, those who work in the domestic sphere are seen as non-threatening workers, as well as outside of reproductive labor. In other words, these workers are not only seen as feminized, but they are also seen as outside of capital because the work they do does not produce a product or surplus value. Instead, the labor of the home is seen as the condition from which capital can proceed. Therefore, domestic workers are ideologically and economically not a threat, but necessary to the economy just the same.

7. The state of Texas is a strong pro-business municipality as the lack of personal, business, and state income tax reveals. Texas is invested in business and private property rather than social services or municipal investment. The results of these material conditions is an ideology that privileges the individual over the communal. It is each individual's right and responsibility to take care of themselves, their property, and their own livelihood, and they need to do this without governmental intervention.

8. Benedict Anderson wrote that citizens imagined commonalities of nations through symbolism, hegemony, and constructed memories. In other words, the cultures of nations are not inherently stable or produced through shared experience.

9. This is what *Branded Bodies* strives to do. It makes visible the imbrication of the economic and cultural and the conjunctures between them. As Stuart Hall has demonstrated, this work must be performed at many different historical and economic moments to insure that Cultural Studies scholars are articulating these connections.

10. The labor structure in H.B. 2012 is an example of Foucauldian biopower. In this case immigrant workers are controlled through exception, and I, as well as Ong, argue that this is a neoliberal means of controlling said population. In other words, in neoliberal governmentality, exceptions are forwarded as a means to regulate and control whole portions of the population. In the example of H.B. 2012 even though it reads as if there are multiple groups being controlled, the exemption is a means to manage both immigrants and citizens within the state of Texas.

11. According to Kenneth Burke in *Rhetoric of Motives*, the ability to create connection through language with someone from whom you are different is not at all the same as persuasion. Instead of creating rhetoric which works toward changing someone's mind or position, identification works toward understanding between two groups or individuals. There is no requirement for either side to change in the process; it is enough to use language to begin to identify through the difference. According to Burke, it is through this process that change can happen. He states: "the individual can identify himself with the character of a surrounding situation, translation one into terms of the other; hence a shift to grander order, the shift from thoughts of one's own individual end to thoughts of a universal end" (16). Burke sees identification as an opportunity for cooperation and social good because it allows for connection through language, not a capitulation because of persuasive tactics. For Burke, identification was rhetoric's greatest necessity, and because man was a creature of language, it had to be attained through language use.

12. There is a long scholarly line of inquiry about the objectification of women and minorities through the "dissecting of their bodies" in media and textual representations. Jean Killbourne, Jackson Katz, Laura Mulvey, and Susan Bordo are just a few of the many scholars who have looked at the ways in which female and raced bodies have been objectified, thus made devoid of subjectivity.

13. According to Michel Foucault a disciplinary society is one that relies on disciplinary structures and people (prisons and police, schools and teachers, churches and clergy) to regulate human behavior. It is within institutions and by those who serve institutions that children are exposed to societal laws and governing rules. From that point on, citizens continue to be educated both explicitly and implicitly by institutions. Foucault's ultimate argument, however, is that eventually people internalize those cultural laws and begin to discipline themselves, so the state institutions do not have to be in all places at all times because most of society is appropriately disciplined (see Foucault's *Discipline and Punish*).

14. Currently, immigration is regulated through quotas. How many documented workers can enter the United States and for how long is determined by corporate need. Then those needs are reviewed and ranked by the U.S. government, and a specific number of visas are provided to the company to hire undocumented workers for a limited time. Therefore, immigration via labor is organized by the numerical need of companies, not the individual need of the immigrants. Those who get documentation are often those who correspond to the number at the top of a list.

15. Since 2008 and the beginning of the most recent recession, there has been discussion in business magazines and journals (Business Weekly, Business Insider.com) and the popular press (MSN.com, Parade.com) about the ethics of using credit scores to vet applicants for jobs. At a time where most jobs have an increase of applicants, employers have seen credit scores as a means to check on "responsibility" and weed out seemingly unserious candidates. Needless to say, this practice has come under much criticism, but it still seems to be a consistent if not uniform practice in many business sectors.

16. Croux, John Joseph. *Symbolic Economies: After Marx and Freud*. Ithaca, NY: Cornell, 1990.

17. In many cases immigrants awaiting asylum decisions and/or deportation appeals are kept in prison-like conditions. Even children have been housed in detention facilities across the world. Immigrants are treated like criminals while they wait to see if they will be fortunate enough to become one of the "others" to which we give access to our country. Furthermore, many western countries (the United States and Australia for example) have been known to change their national borders in moments of "emergency" to prevent asylum seekers from gaining access to the nation-state.

18. Klein argues that the term neoliberal economics is too vague and does not specify who benefits from and whose interests are served by our current governmental economic protocols. She believes that corporatist economics is more descriptive of the true nature of the economic system in place today. I, however, decline to take on Klein's terminology because I feel that corporatist economics only grants definition to the power base that benefits from the economic system and can easily occlude those who are positioned to serve as material labor for the corporate system.

19. The greatest irony here is that during times of "shock" the public returns to the social contract in the hopes that their civil liberties will be protected and honored by their government. Yet it is that very moment that the government is using the public's desire for protection to erode those civil liberties and the social contract upon which they have come to rely. A strong example of this exchange is post–9/11 America and the development of The Patriot Act. The legislation was "sold" to the American public as necessary to protect them. All the while it stripped us of many basic civil liberties in the name of that protection.

20. So neoliberal ideology does not produce its subjects by interpolating them into symbolically anchored identities (structured according to conventions of gender, race,

work, and national citizenship). Instead, it enjoins subjects to develop our creative potential and cultivate our individuality (Dean 66–67).

21. This is how the justification for the invasion of Iraq 2003 was created.

22. In her book *Networking Arguments*, Dingo discusses how rhetoric is formed through neoliberal linkages that cross both global and economic borders. She examines policy and NGO public exchanges to demonstrate how neoliberal culture has created conditions for changes in rhetorical practice.

23. A palimpsestic reading, according to M. Jacqui Alexander, who works to define ideology as inflected and mobile in her book, *Pedagogies of Crossing,* allows scholars to begin to view ideological practice as unbounded by history and nation. It is a shift necessary for understanding ideology as transnational in its very conception. Alexander defines the transnational not only spatially but also temporally. She asserts that our current state ideologies are not developments from historical moments. Rather they are carried throughout time shifting and mutating (but not becoming wholly different) in particular circumstances. She uses the term "ideological traffic" to reveal the ways in which the same ideologies can be seen functioning in historical spaces, as well as current ones.

24. Beginning with Aristotle's *Rhetoric*, logos has been central to rhetorical practice. Even Quintillian's "Good Man Speaking Well" was premised on the idea that man had the ability to construct persuasive arguments logically and ethically. The use of emotion (pathos) was often seen as base or a way to undermine the work of the rhetoric.

25. Corrina Bonshek articulates Deleuze's theory of intensity in relationship to her and Anna Bonsek's artwork *reverie 1 (2002).* She states: "Deleuze uses the concept of 'intensity' to describe elements at the limits of perception. He describes intensities as pure differences, a form of ontological difference that gives rise to 'actual' or perceived entities. As qualities of pure difference, intensities are virtual, though nonetheless real. They cannot be directly perceived. Rather, as Deleuze suggests, they can only be felt, sensed or perceived in the 'quality' they give rise to."

TWO

Branding the Family

U.S. Protectionism and the Tie that Binds

BRANDING THE NATION: IT'S ALL IN THE FAMILY

On March 14, 2007, Salon.com, an independent-liberal online magazine, ran an article by Garrison Keillor, host of National Public Radio's (NPR) "A Prairie Home Companion." The article was titled "Stating the Obvious" and contained the tagline quote "Nature doesn't care about the emotional well-being of older people. It's about the continuation of the species—in other words, children." And it is the rhetoric of "children first" or children as the representatives of the family upon which Keillor draws throughout the piece.[1] However, Keillor does not fully problematize that rhetoric.[2] Instead, through his commitment to the "good of the children," he reifies the image of the post–World War II nuclear family in which children were constructed as central to the family and society. Keillor states, "I grew up the child of a mixed-gender marriage that lasted until death parted them, and I could tell you all about how good that is for children, and you could pay me whatever you think it's worth." Keillor draws upon discourses of the nuclear family, which I will discuss at length in this chapter, to emphasize the centrality of heteronormative values to the construction of the traditional U.S. family.[3] Even though he utilizes politically correct language like "mixed-gendered" and notes that some folks will not consider his opinion of much worth, Keillor still establishes a family as a man and woman with child(ren) as the normative family model from which he will proceed.

Even when Keillor acknowledges gay fathers within his essay, it is clear that he is concerned with the inappropriate appearance of these men. Instead of concentrating on gay marriage, he turns his attention to

27

the dress and demeanor of gay fathers. He states: "If [gay men] want to be accepted as couples and daddies, however, the flamboyance may have to be brought under control. Parents are supposed to stand in the back and not wear chartreuse pants and black polka-dot shirts" (1). Keillor's critique may seem to mitigate the conservatism surrounding gay marriage and families. After all, he is positing that gay men are indeed fathers. However, his admonishment of the dress and attributes of "gay men" is couched in the same terms as his critiques of non-monogamy. Keillor sees these fathers as non-standard, with the standard being heterosexual men who don't wear chartreuse pants and polka-dots. Therefore, he is reifying stereotypical images of who is allowed to be a family man and who is not. A gay man is only allowed to be a father if he looks like a heterosexual one.

The rhetoric of the breakdown of the heteronormative nuclear family—mother, father, child(ren)—circulates throughout Keillor's piece. It matters not if a parent is gay or straight, but a parent needs to look and act like a parent. Because of Keillor's upbringing, those parents are defined as monogamous and heterosexual. Furthermore, those parents need to be intelligible as U.S. citizens, and through his final example Keillor solidifies this question by noting who is (or looks like) a U.S. citizen. He states: "Fifteen different languages and dialects spoken in the school, a teacher told me. In my lifetime, the potato fields had been developed into tract housing for World War II vets and now a landing site for immigrants and their second-graders, most of whom ventured into English only a year ago" (1). The immigrant children of whom Keillor writes are not the same as the children he discusses earlier in his piece. Instead of a lecture about how parents should treat these children, his tone changes to one of longing for his "lifetime" and concern for these non-English-speaking immigrants. But his concern does not seem to reach to their familial situations. Instead, the immigrant children, much like the gay father, are a threat to his nostalgic vision of the white heteronormative U.S. family.

Each group that Keillor discusses throughout his essay—from serial-monogamous extended families, to flamboyant gay fathers, to immigrant children—challenges his vision of the American family. The American family is in decline, and there are notable reasons as to why this is—changing family structures, homosexuality, and immigration. And those who come to represent these changes—the single welfare mother, the gay dad, and the immigrant—become threatening, if not a direct threat, to the status of family. These brands, even in Keillor's description, are not real individuals. There are no anecdotes about or quotations from individuals here. Instead, they are monolithic categories that serve, much like the notion of a forgotten American family, to help us define who are acceptable families and who are threats to that very structure.

As discussed throughout chapter one, branding works because it draws on sublimated economic and social anxieties. Currently, it is forwarded as a means to simplify complex relationships—whether they are economic, political, or interpersonal. As the Keillor example demonstrates through his branding of "family," even though the brands are drawn from implicit histories of racism, misogyny, homophobia, and sexism, they are used to forward a "simpler" vision of the American family. The threats to this version of the family are often reminiscent of Keillor's constructions of familial change—the immigrant and GLBT body both function as brands against whom we can define the normative American family. This chapter, then, will discuss how the branding of "the family" flattens the deep material differences between those who are seen as part of that normative family and those who are not.

The notion of the fragility of the national family—a family that is in need of constant protection—is at the heart of the family values discourse that has asserted itself as the cornerstone of neoliberal national identity.[4] If the U.S. family is under attack, then the United States itself is, as well; and it is the sexually free, homosexual, and immigrant populations who are constructed as the most eminent threats. By identifying the enemy of the family, the enemies of the state have also been identified.

I began with a discussion of Keillor's brief essay to demonstrate the ways in which narratives of sexual orientation, sexuality, and immigration intersect to provide a picture of a U.S. family that is changing and thus provoking anxiety. Even if Keillor is attempting to expose these narratives as falsely totalizing, his movement from sexual practice, to sexuality, to immigration, to the nostalgia for the wide frontier demonstrates the ways in which these narratives are central to how we see ourselves as Americans. By taking a relatively conservative tone in an independent Web magazine and on a radio show on a widely broadcast radio syndicate, both of which self-identify as liberal, Keillor demonstrates how the story of the attack on the heteronormative American family has circulated well past the confines of the conservative media and has permeated our cultural logics.

Furthermore, as Keillor's essay shows, these discussions not only name the changes in family structure; through negation, they romanticize a vision of a "whole" and "unified" family that is reminiscent of the nuclear family as defined post–World War II. This romanticized family is not a material reality because of divorce, job loss, and decreased governmental spending over the past sixty years. The primacy of the nuclear family has deep ties to the development of the suburbs and the removal of women from the workforce post–World War II. According to Andres Duany, the suburbs were developed not only to justify the continued construction of the nationwide highway system that began during World War II; they were also a site where families could become models of consumption (*Suburban Nation*). Thus, the nuclear family, where the

mother stayed home with the children and had her own home to keep
and maintain while the father worked, became central to the narrative of
postwar family life. This vision gave women something to "do" in maintaining a "positive home space" for their hardworking husbands, and it
allowed them to become framed as "active consumer citizens" (*A Consumer's Republic* iiv). So, instead of serving their country in the factories,
they could now serve in the catalogue and grocery stores.

A father, mother, and child(ren) living in a single family home, prefer-
ably in the suburbs, is the familial image that Keillor puts forth as in
danger. While it may seem as if it is purely in the interest of nostalgia and
values, it is also in the interest of U.S. politics and economics that the
nuclear family remain intact. These families were not only defined by
their configuration, but also by how they upheld the standards of U.S.
citizen-ness. In other words, these families were not only ideological constructions, but also economic and political ones. As such, they had a
specific job to do within the cultural imaginary of the United States. They
not only defined who could be a family, but also who was an appropriate
citizen.

Therefore, when the "U.S. family" is branded, not all families are intelligible within that brand. For Grace Kyungwon Hong, this is the mark-
er of neoliberal capitalism. Drawing on arguments by Reddy and Berlant,
she articulates the connections between capitalism and affect in connection with the brand of the family:

> "[F]amily is a category of normativization for the citizen-as-capitalist,
> but only insofar as it is simultaneously a category of exploitation for
> the noncitizen immigrant and the racialized citizen poor. In this con-
> text, the racialized poor are rendered vulnerable so as to produce them
> as a form of surplus labor, but they are also abjected as backward,
> homophobic, and patriarchal as a way to render them as morally bank-
> rupt and exclude them from a privileged liberal subjecthood: existen-
> tially surplus" ("Existentially Surplus" 94).

For Hong, the commercialization of the family does more than merely
stratify the nation-state based on classed, racial, and sexual differences.
Instead, it creates subjects who are surplus to the project of neoliberalism
wherein those who are consumer-citizen-*subjects* are characterized as ac-
cepting of difference.

This de-subjectifying of seemingly homophobic or non-racially sensi-
tive citizens helps to reify the image of the generous multicultural state
discussed in chapter one. However, this de-subjectifying of certain
groups, whether they are citizens or not, also allows for particular bodies
to be marked as "other-other"—and therefore threatening and in need of
expulsion. The brand of the family does not prevent these binaries, but
instead it fuels them by identifying certain families who are to be feared,
and therefore not protected. To demonstrate how the brand of the family

and the branding of threats work to establish who can and cannot be accepted by the nation-state, I will look at two pieces of GLBT and immigration legislation in 1996 (the Defense of Marriage Act and the Illegal Immigration Reform and Immigrant Responsibility Act), as well as the media coverage surrounding them. Then I will analyze two pieces of 2006 legislation, the Family Marriage Act and H.R. 4437, and media discourse surrounding them, in order to show how branding the family is not merely about families, but also about communities and the United States as a whole.

By assembling these pieces of legislation, I can begin to show the ways in which the later post–9/11 pieces of legislation represent a rise in the affective intensity surrounding the branding of protection. By defining which families need protection and which do not, legislators and the media are occluding the conversations of material and historic realities. Thus, this chapter will demonstrate how branding is not only present, but works to occlude a full understanding of the history of protection throughout media and legislation. It is the branding of threats that creates a push and pull between generosity and fear. Much like discussion of Hage's "gift of citizenship" in chapter one, U.S. families want protection both at home and abroad. However, how the "other" is branded determines the delivery of that protection—the expulsion or assimilation of the other. In the case of branded threats, often the foreign and domestic threats work to form a comprehensive state of fear from which the family must be protected. The branding of the family, then, does not account for the economic or political struggles that most American families are facing; instead, U.S. public policies recast both external and internal threats from which the American family is in dire need of protection.

THE GOOD CITIZEN/THE GOOD FAMILY

Although the family is not a new term within political discourse,[5] the shift from liberal to neoliberal governmentality takes the brand of the family out of the realm of the instrumental, or organizational, and puts it into the realm of creating affect. Lauren Berlant traces the beginning of this shift in discourse to the early 1980s in the early stages of Reaganomics (*The Queen of America Goes to Washington City*).[6] Since then, American citizens have been steadily losing their jobs and their standard of living because of inflation and cuts to social welfare. But instead of rebelling against the government or voting their interests,[7] a significant portion of the American public has voted in the interest of American family values—the one thing that the GOP could give them with which to define themselves in times of economic struggle and/or loss. Berlant states: "No longer valuing personhood as something directed toward public life, con-

temporary nationalist ideology recognizes a public good only in a particularly constricted nation of simultaneously lived private worlds" (5). She
names this the "intimate public sphere," and it follows the same logic(s)
of personal responsibility noted by Duggan and Ong. However, Berlant
sutures these logics to specific debates that engage intimate issues. Instead of focusing on larger political (or public) debates, it is organized
around private matters through debates of family values.

In other words, the intimate public sphere is concerned with private
qua personal debates that traditionally have been discussed within the
home, not public spaces. A good example of how the intimate has entered the public sphere is President Clinton's impeachment trial in 1999.
Clinton was accused of lying to the American public, but his lie was not
in the context of a political or economic scandal. Instead, he lied to the
country about his sexual practices in the Oval Office with a woman other
than his wife. By attempting to impeach him based solely on this intimate
transgression, Congress and the American media suggested that Clinton's behavior as a husband and father was just as important as how he
governed the country, thus collapsing the differences between family/
private practice and career/public practice. The introduction of private
behavior into political debates allows the discussion of job success to shift
to a discussion of the success of one's private relationships. Clinton's
impeachment trial demonstrates that family matters are now the province of the state.

Part of the work of the rhetoric surrounding the Clinton impeachment
was the mobilization by the right wing of the notions of appropriate
behavior for a family man and über-citizen—the president. By focusing
on Clinton's sexual indiscretions, right-wing pundits and other political
groups were able to mobilize the rhetoric of family values as a means to
define not only the position of the president but also what is valued by
American citizens.[8] In other words, the family, and appropriate sexual
behavior therein, became not only a cause for impeachment, but also a
means of defining what it meant to be a true American. M. Jacqui Alexander discusses the ways in which nation-states not only use legislation to
define the family as a heterosexual one but also use membership and
adherence to that form of family as the defining terms of citizenship.[9]
Alexander states that, rhetorically, citizenship functions as a means of
underwriting of the project of nation building in ways that paradoxically
render the boundaries of the nation-state as fixed by designating loyal
heterosexual citizenship among normative hierarchies of race, gender,
and class that guard the boundaries of the nation-state from sexual per-
versity and from certain classes of immigrants who ostensibly undo the
nation's interests by relying on public assistance and whose movement
across the borders of the nation must therefore be curtailed. (247)

Alexander discusses how the Personal Responsibility and Work
Opportunity Reconciliation Act of 1996, the Illegal Immigration Reform

and Immigrant Responsibility Act of 1996, and the Defense of Marriage Act work together to build America's national identity. Yet these pieces of legislation are rarely examined in connection with one another. Instead, these laws are seen as responding to particular issues at home and abroad, and therefore, are not examined in the context of the complex ideological web of gender, race, class, sexuality, and immigrant status that Alexander sees working through them. These laws, however, do interanimate one another, presenting a narrative of the nation as being under siege by immigrants and sexual minorities. This can be seen in the ways these laws utilize the brand of the family to assert a particular U.S. familial identity that needs protection in order to shore up the nation as a whole.

The family, then, becomes not just any family. It becomes a brand. As I discussed in chapter one, it is at once used to affectively engage citizens' emotions while masking all the material relationships denoted above. The brand of the family is mobilized to define an American national identity. It is through the assemblage of the brands of the family and those from whom the family needs protection (immigrant and GLBT bodies) that, much like Hage sees in Australia, the U.S. public forms a branded identity. The right-wing political parties and other groups have branded the family and mobilized the rhetoric of home invasion and threat in order to define who needs to be protected from whom.

In other words, by invoking threats to the family which support the heteronormative branding of the family, political rhetoric serves as a means not only to create affective identification with those who need protection, but also to create affective intensities around that from which we need protection. Queer theorist Janet Jakobsen discusses the ways in which values and capital are complicit in using bodies to reaffirm "the American identity" in our neoliberal, transnational economic moment. For her, the bodies of immigrants and the bodies of GLBT people are also often used to shore up the nation. Jakobsen states:

> Talk of "family values" signals a reconstruction of American citizenship that regulates and distinguishes those Americans who deserve the rights and benefits of citizenship from those who do not—whether they are actually U.S. citizens or not—hence, in part, the anxieties about immigration and so-called illegal aliens, who threaten the borders of the United States even as those boundaries are weakened (and penetration is welcomed?) by a queer subversion from within. (177)

Jakobsen discusses how the "sexual deviant" and "illegal immigrant" are separate but equal threats that come from the inside and outside of the nation respectively. This is important to note because the threat of sexuality is a threat that is often constructed as coming from the interior of the home or family, whereas the threat of immigration comes from outside the national borders, thus outside the family unit. Even though these two threats are constructed differently, they both still function rhetorically together to present a picture of the family under siege. Together they solidify the urgent nature of the threat.

This urgency is created through the use of affective intensity,[10] as discussed in chapter one, whereby the rhetorical production of the immigrant or GLBT other works to create an emotional reaction based on historically grounded and biased claims about immigrant and GLBT bodies. No longer are those claims made directly. Instead, we see them marshaled through the branding of the family, which can and sometimes does include "acceptable" immigrant and GLBT bodies. Therefore it is not the *classification* of immigrant or GLBT that is the threat in and of itself. Instead, it is the ways in which these histories are rhetorically invoked, through the use of palimpsestic imprints within the brand of family that enables these brands to create notions of threat and danger that might be even offensive today.

Both immigrant and GLBT bodies are branded as threats, and within certain rhetorical contexts, they become unregulated; they do not "fit in" with the standards of Americanness that permeate "the family." Therefore, they become nonstandard invaders of the home who are material threats to families, and especially children. Because of these threats, the United States must provide legal regulations in order to stop or penalize those responsible for the threat. It is not only the media coverage, then, that participates in branding of bodies; legislation and policy are also created with the protection of families in mind.

THE BRANDING OF PROTECTION: THE LAW OF THE FAMILY

While implementing some key protections for American families, the Illegal Immigration Reform and Immigrant Responsibility Act of 1996 (IIRAIRA) limited the rights of immigrant families in profound ways. Some of the newest regulations under the IIRAIRA imposed heavier penalties for legal immigrants who preferred to migrate between the United States and their home country for seasonal employment rather than pursue U.S. citizenship. Additionally, the government specified that immigrants reapplying or renewing their visa status had to do it in person and after a full medical examination by a United States-registered doctor.[11] Finally, the IIRAIRA imposed a ten-year exile for immigrants who did not meet these requirements prior to the expiration of their visas. What this meant for documented immigrants was that student and work visas were no longer the answer, and if they had enough access and money, they would need to become U.S. citizens in order to live and/or travel in the ways in which they had become accustomed.

But the legislation was not just for those "other" families; it was also a means of legislating who was considered a valid family both in the United States and beyond. By defining spaces and bodies that exist outside of the normative definition of citizenship and nationhood, U.S. legislators are working rhetorically to define the nation-state.[12] The IIRAIRA focused on citizenship by restricting rights and privileges on the basis of non-citizenship status. In fact, the immigrants who were here in the country on legal visas lost more rights than anyone else. Therefore, even though the title of the legislation places the illegal immigrant as the first subject of the reform, it was the legal immigrants who needed to learn their new responsibilities to the state. Much like the exceptions in H.B. 2012 discussed in chapter one, IIRAIRA underclassed a whole class of immigrants, but it was done in the name of protection. Although these immigrants are documented and meet the standards set forth by the United States, they will never be granted citizenship, because it is not in the economic interest of the United States to do so. Instead, the nation develops reasons to see immigrants as threats who must be regulated both inside and outside the nation-state.

IIRAIRA works to define who is legal within the nation, but it also focuses on those bodies external to the nation-state regardless of their legal status. So, immigrants who consistently leave the country to return are a new kind of threat, no matter how up-to-date their paperwork may be. No longer is it just the illegal immigrant who is threatening the safety of the United States. Now the legal immigrant who leaves and returns, not making the United States their new permanent home, is a threat as well.

Historically, immigrants both inside and outside U.S. borders have been constructed as threats during times of war or economic uncertainty. Whether it be through the Alien and Sedition Acts, which detailed who could be expelled from the country and for what reason, or the development of state specific legislation, like Texas's H.B. 2012, immigrants both documented or undocumented have often been misconstrued as the cause of economic and political instability within the United States. As I discussed in chapter one, many of these state mandates against immigration are in response to a view of immigrants as threats to the already declining economic status of the state. As such, immigrants are constructed as threats to the economy and culture in times of economic downturn.

Syd Lindsley argues that the reason that immigration legislation in California, in particular, during the 1990s seemed to target women, children, and families was because of the changing demographics of migration. During the 1990s, women and children were entering the country at a much higher rate than previously noted. The shift in migration patterns was in response to neoliberal economic trends that created conditions for privatized labor within the United States. Many of the jobs available during the 1990s were primarily connected to homecare—nanny, gardening, housekeeping—and were considered feminized sites of labor. Additionally, several pieces of immigration legislation limited the patterns of "family" migration by restricting spousal immigration; increasing fees and tightening restrictions for who can become a citizen; restricting pre-natal care to only certain levels of documented immigrants; and ending bilingual education, welfare, medical, and state service support for un-documented immigrants. Each of these laws made it more difficult for immigrant women, children, and families to migrate to the United States and remain.

Leaving aside costs of international travel, which are prohibitive for many, new laws such as the United States Patriot Act, and the mobiliza-tion of Operation Gatekeeper are limiting who can enter the country and who can stay, as well as determining who must leave. National borders may be getting more restrictive when it comes to the exchange of foreign bodies, but those same flows are open wider than ever when it comes to international corporate business and trade. This tension impacts immi-grant families because it determines who can stay together and who can be identified as an acceptable family by the U.S. nation-state.

Avtar Brah notes that by limiting how many Mexican workers can enter the United States, what kind of worker can enter, and who is al-lowed to enter with them—spouse, child(ren), extended family—immi-gration laws that limit workers who work for low wages in the lower tiers of the labor market are helping to keep the U.S. economy going. The delicate balance between economics, social beliefs, industry, and the identification of the "other" all influence this site of migration and ex-change of both people and industry. The reason that immigrant families are kept out of America is not their overextension of the U.S. economy. Rather it is because of the backlash created from industry moving into Mexico so that these industries can pay less for the labor of Mexican workers. Even though factory jobs cannot be replaced with the salary from service industry work, many blue collar Americans resent the fact that Mexican workers are taking their jobs at home and abroad. As a result, the immigrants who do enter the country are constructed as threats—those who will steal our jobs—and by extension, their families are seen as threats that need to be regulated as well.

This fear of immigrants is extrapolated beyond the actual borders of the United States. IIRAIRA uses the brand of the family to articulate the fear of what is outside the United States early in the legislation—even before the stipulations of who can come in, who can stay, and who must be expelled. In section 235A 5 a, b, there is clear discussion of the protec-tion of the families of U.S. citizens when outside of the country. It states:

> CONDITIONS.—Prior to the establishment of a preinspection station, the Attorney General, in consultation with the Secretary of State, shall ensure that—

a. employees of the United States stationed at the preinspection station and their accompanying family members will receive appropriate protection;

b. such employees and their families will not be subject to unreasonable risks to their welfare and safety. (Sec. 235A. Preinspection at foreign airports)

Preinspection stations are much like customs areas within airports. However, unlike customs areas outside of the United States that are staffed and controlled by local governments, U.S. Immigration and Customs Enforcement (ICE) employees who would check visa and passport paperwork for foreign nationals attempting to fly into the United States would staff these stations. In other words, the United States would extend the policing of its borders into other national territories where there are high percentages of immigrants or asylum seekers coming to the United States.

According to Amy Kaplan, preinspection stations function as a means to secure the brand (to use my terminology) of the "U.S. homeland." She claims that the invocation of homeland, although contradictory to many of the United States's central tenets—manifest destiny, class mobility, meritocracy—holds a powerful notion of rhetorically constructed place. In other words, by invoking the brand of "homeland," the United States can, and does, assert its national boundaries, even when outside its own legal jurisdiction.

> "Yet it does this not simply by stopping foreigners at the borders, but by continually redrawing those boundaries everywhere throughout the nation, between Americans who can somehow claim the United States as their native land, their birthright, and immigrants and those who look to homelands elsewhere, who can be rendered inexorably foreign" (Kaplan 87).

By consistently redrawing borders, policing immigrants within and without, the United States is able to give the impression that their nation, and subsequently, their laws extend far beyond the borders of its nation.

This practice in connection with preinspection stations does not seem egregious, but the same logic can be extrapolated to detainment facilities on foreign soil, thus expanding the military and policing arm of the United States with little intervention. Kaplan discusses the military detention center at Guantanamo as a site wherein the United States acts in an official capacity without invoking national or international law. This space has been critically examined because of its seeming lack of adherence to any nation's oversight. Instead, it is a non-place (to borrow a term from Marc Augé) where no international or national laws pertain. For Kaplan, Guantanamo is a site where the invocation of "homeland" supersedes the legal responsibilities of the nation-state. She sees this as a development within neoliberal globalization; however, there are other scholars who see the rift between ideological discourse and material legal reality as just another development in the "U.S. Imperial Project" (Braziel "One Indispensable Nation").

In connection with preinspection stations, though, Guantanamo becomes an extreme example of these non-juridical spaces in which the United States creates its own national identity through the processes and actions it commits therein. By creating offshore legal checkpoints across the globe, the United States is both recognizing the porousness of its national borders *and* extending its authority beyond the borders of the nation. But the presence of U.S. citizens and their families at these sites tells a different tale. The family in this case is the portable reminder that the U.S. ICE agents are not global citizens. They are U.S. citizens who will be "appropriately protected" while abroad just as if they were in their home country. This rhetoric is significant because, much like the rhetoric surrounding the Clinton impeachment, it is a means to demonstrate the boundaries of who is a U.S. citizen and who is not, through the mobilization of protection. Even while outside of the United States, U.S. citizens must be protected when they are working to protect the United States on foreign soil.

In fact, I would argue that the IIRAIRA reestablishes the centrality of the American family in order to reaffirm the U.S. nation-state. By extending its jurisdiction outside of its national borders, there is the image of the United States reestablishing itself as an imperial power across the globe. However, the United States is not attempting to change local or international laws. Instead the phrase "unreasonable risks" reveals that outside the United States the level of threat is heightened, and therefore U.S. families need more protection than ever when in foreign lands. The American family becomes the stand-in for the United States and the brand of normalcy in the space of the international. The absence of cooperation between or even the mere mention of foreign national policing and protection reveals the United States's move to establish its own protection and authority. And through domestic policy, the United States reiterates that its primary concern is the protection of U.S. families at home and abroad. The family is scripted into law as a means to nation-build, even on foreign soil.

But threats to families do not only come from outside the U.S. border. Threats can also come from the homeland itself. It is through the articulation of these threats that the state can further limit who can be a citizen while reinforcing the normal state of the citizen family. IIRAIRA solidifies Berlant's claim about the intimate public sphere not only through its articulation of protection for U.S. families abroad, but also in its domestic violence section, which is new to immigration law. The presence of a domestic violence policy not only helps to establish the family as a key unit of relation that needs to be protected, but also begins to regulate these relationships by articulating particular familial positions: "parent," "spouse," "child," and "relative." The use of normative categories of family membership serves to restrict who can be protected from abuse. This protection is limited to those in a family unit that is identifiable and normative. In other words, by using traditional terms to define the ways in which abuse is recognized, the IIRAIRA establishes regulations that only protect against abuse that happens between parents, children, and spouses and/or those connected to the household in some fashion.

In the section titled "Entrants and Immigrant Violators," the subsection "Exception for Certain Battered Women and Children" clearly articulates who is in the family by defining who can be harmed in the family. It states:

> (a) The alien has been battered or subjected to extreme cruelty by a spouse or parent, or by a member of the spouse's or parent's family residing in the same household as the alien and the spouse or parent consented or acquiesced to such battery of cruelty, or (b) the alien's child has been battered or subjected to extreme cruelty by a spouse or parent of the alien (without the active participation of the alien in the battery or cruelty) or by a member of the spouse's or parent's family residing in the same household as the alien when the spouse or parent consented to or acquiesced in such battery or cruelty and the alien did not actively participate in such battery or cruelty. (sec. 301)

The use of the terms "spouse," "parent," "child," and "household," much like the domestic violence law they articulate, creates an image of a traditional family where members are legally committed to one another—as spouses or children.[13] In addition to being traditional filial relationships that establish a traditional value-laden image of family, these relationships are guarded by particular legal rights. Through the domestic violence addendum, these rights are spelled out quite clearly in relation to immigration law. Therefore, the immigrants who are just like us—married with children—must be afforded the same rights and privileges as U.S. families. Through this stipulation, the state becomes both benevolent to victims within families *and* unambiguous that the family is natural and not cultural. After all, if even immigrants fall into these filial norms, our conception of family must be rearticulated in connection with issues of immigration and citizenship in order to remind us who can be citizens and who we can protect.

The IIRAIRA's use of "families," "spouses," and "children" is not new in immigration legislation. In fact, in her queer analysis of the 1798 Naturalization Act, Siobhan Somerville shows how sexualized bodies are deeply connected through the process of naturalization. These terms are marked and carry the palimpsestic inflection of past utterances even in their new context. As Somerville discusses, these brands have been heterosexualized throughout the history of immigration law and discourse. Although she discusses how the process of naturalization had a chance to "queer" citizenship by making it a choice rather than a natural state granted through birth, she ultimately claims that possibility was quickly squelched with the addendum to the naturalization law which stated that any child born while living in the United States, regardless of the citizenship status of his/her parents, would be considered a U.S. citizen. For Somerville, this was a way of reining in citizenship by reaffirming heterosexual procreation as its primary condition.

Following Somerville's assertions about the primacy of heterosexuality to citizenship, I suggest that the presence of a domestic violence statute in IIRAIRA allows for a gendered reading of the law itself. Most discussions and legal discourse surrounding domestic violence are put forth as a means to protect women and children from men. Therefore, even though there are no assignments of gender in IIRAIRA, with the exception of women in the title of the clause, the terms "spouse" and "children" call up traditional ideas of family and procreation, which have been normalized in state discourses as heterosexual. However, the brand of the family is central to the discourse of protection because it represents a significant shift from what Somerville describes. The heterosexual family is no longer just the basis for citizenship; it is also the rhetorical construction from which citizens should gain their identity. It is through the notion of protection, in this case, that the family can gain legitimacy in the eyes of the law.[14] Who can and cannot, who should and should not, be protected are all determined on the basis of behaviors and affective intensities that generate empathy from both those who are already citizens, and those who want to be citizens.

The heterosexual family becomes the central instrument of citizenship and in the IIRAIRA example, the heterosexual family is the primary source of identification for U.S. citizens. In order to *feel* as if they belong, citizens come to identify with the construction of the heterosexual family. IIRAIRA alludes to the family as a procreative one through the discussion of biological connection, but it does not specifically speak to the ways in which family members may be U.S. citizens, nor does it specifically name the gender of each spouse or member of the household. But that is because the IIRAIRA did not need to define the term "spouse." That definition was already circulating throughout public discourse because of the Defense of Marriage Act of 1996 (DOMA).

DOMA functioned under the same paradigms of protection as IIRAIRA; however, its main focus was not the threats coming from outside the United States, but rather those who were already at home. In addition to solidifying state autonomy by allowing states not to recognize unions and marriages between couples performed outside of that state's boundaries,[15] DOMA also clearly defined the terms "marriage" and "spouse" in order to limit any confusion as to who could be or could not be a spouse in a marriage. The legislation states:

In determining the meaning of any Act of Congress, or of ruling, regulation, or interpretation of the various administrative bureaus and
agencies of the United States, the word "marriage" means only a legal
union between one man and one woman as husband and wife, and the
word "spouse" of the opposite sex who is a husband or a wife. (Sec 3,
H.R. 3396)

The language of DOMA itself is fairly clear, but the ramifications of that
language and the fact that this piece of legislation redefined "any Act of
Congress, ruling, regulation, or interpretation" that contained the words
"marriage" and "spouse" are what make it so powerful. By regulating
these particular terms, DOMA ensured that all laws using these terms,
such as the IIRAIRA, would have to use the definitions established by
DOMA. Therefore, by discussing issues of domestic violence in terms of
"spouse" or "child" or "marriage" or "household," the IIRAIRA did not
have to clarify the gender and/or sexual orientation of the families because it was done in another piece of legislation not directly connected to
it.

MEDIATING THE FAMILY: AN EQUAL OPPORTUNITY BRAND

In the debates surrounding IIRAIRA and DOMA, both mainstream and
alternative presses use the same rhetorical construction—the family—to
debate the effects and consequences of specific legislation. Once again,
there is the move toward affective identification. Statements made in
both right-wing and progressive publications reveal the ways in which
the family is central to citizenship. A right-wing representative in favor of
DOMA characterized the changes to the family: "'The flames of hedon-
ism, the flames of narcissism, the flames of self-centered morality are
licking at the very foundations of our society, the family unit,' said Rep.
Bob Barr, R-GA, the bill's sponsor" (AP). Compare that quotation to a
simple statement made by Jake Bernstein reporting on the representative
responsible for the IIRAIRA in the alternative press publication *The Texas
Observer*: "The comprehensive 1996 legislation [Rep. Lamar Smith R-TX]
authored also targeted legal permanent residents, many who had been in
the country for decades and had U.S. citizen children and spouses" (4).

Although the quote from Bernstein is not nearly as vitriolic as Barr's, it
does establish empathy for immigrants through their possible filial connections. First, there is the term "spouse," which we know because of
DOMA only denotes a heterosexual coupling. He is attempting to criti-
cize the IIRAIRA because it separates families with children. There is an
assumption that we should be sympathetic to immigrants as long as their
families mirror the U.S. heteronormative family. However, within his
comment, the immigrant families are not only acceptable because they
are recognizable families, but because they are already legally attached to

the United States. The immigrants discussed in Bernstein's quote are already part of the national family because they have married someone who is already a citizen. Therefore, much like the families abroad in the early sections of the IIRAIRA, they should be afforded the same protections of U.S. citizen families. This logic not only reifies the centrality of U.S. citizenship, but it also reinforces Bush's mandate of personal responsibility. These immigrants and citizens are helping to define the nation-state through their individual actions, not their interaction with national law. IIRAIRA is yet another instance where U.S. law is following neoliberal practices and focusing on the private sphere.

Due to the changes in immigration law preventing immigrants from easily bringing other family members into the country after a prescribed amount of time regardless of their citizenship status, many immigrant families have been separated. Bernstein's comment in the alternative liberal press reminds us who the families in need of protection are—the ones where at least one member is a U.S. citizen. Even though immigrants have experienced grievous affronts because of neoliberal economic practice, including new felony charges and employment restrictions, Bernstein argues that the image of someone separated from his/her spouse and children is what humanizes immigrants and makes them a cause worth fighting for. In this instance, being branded a family member makes an immigrant an intelligible subject within the nation. The family rhetorically becomes the point wherein affective identification can be created. In other words, it is not economic and/or citizenship or consumer status that works to help immigrants become intelligible. Instead, the notion that immigrants are caring, heterosexual families, *just like us,* works rhetorically as a means to create identification through affect.

For example, Dan P. Danilov in his article in the *Northwest Asian Weekly* gives a lengthy narrative of how the new immigration law will affect an immigrant who marries a U.S. citizen. In his article, he writes:

> As a simple example, suppose "Alice" entered the United States on February 15, 1993 with a B-1/B-2 Temporary Non-Immigrant Business/ Visitor's Visa for an authorized period of six months. Accordingly, her visa status in the United States expired on August 15, 1993. Further, Alice also accepted employment in the United States until the present time. On October 7, 1996, Alice married her boyfriend, a U.S. citizen. Inasmuch as Alice was not in legal status in the United States for three years, there is now a question of her eligibility for Adjustment of Status to a Lawful Permanent Resident without departing the United States by reason of her marriage to a U.S. citizen spouse. (14)

Alice's credentials to become a U.S. citizen are directly tied to marriage even though she has worked in the United States for the past three years. Once again, there is a privileging of the creation of family through marriage that is fully supported by immigration law. But the crux of Alice's problem is the fact that she could be deported for ten years because she has been out of status for the past three years. The hardship here is that the couple has to decide, should they risk her deportation and have Alice apply for citizenship? Or should she forfeit those rights she now can claim because of her marriage and not run that risk? It is Danilov's point that this should not be a decision the family of a U.S. citizen should have to face.

Danilov's attempt to create a family allegory to try to personalize the legal ramifications of the current legislation shows how deeply family matters in these debates, and his argument reveals the intimate public sphere's deep attachment to the logics of neoliberalism—especially personal responsibility. Arguing for the humanity of immigrants on the basis of filial relationships masks the material economic and political issues facing immigrants in the United States. There are many such articles in opposition to both the IIRAIRA and DOMA that attempt to use the family to create empathy. What is very telling is that they all discuss the ways these new legislative limitations will disrupt families. The implication is that even though these families have been marked as different through legislation, they are still families just like us who are in need of the protection, not ostracization, of the state. But no matter how many families are utilized to decry the unjust legislation that was passed in 1996, the fact remains that not all people become part of intelligible families, and not all families are brand-able in service of the U.S. national imaginary. Those who cannot be branded as a heteronormative family are seen as threats to the nation who must be expelled. The rhetoric of IIRAIRA and DOMA make that very clear.

FAMILIES, COMMUNITIES, AND NATIONS: THE INTENSITY OF POST–9/11 DISCOURSE

The branding of who can be a family, and thus receive the rights and privileges afforded to them and who cannot, did not end with the passage of DOMA and IIRAIRA. In fact, in 2006, we can see the same patterns of branding emerge in both immigration reform (H.R. 4437) and reforms around the term "marriage" (Federal Marriage Act [FMA]). However, even though the terms circulate in similar ways, these two pieces of legislation did not pass the House of Representatives or the Senate, and therefore did not become law like their counterparts did ten years earlier. It was argued by most that these pieces of legislation, in addition to being unduly harsh in their construction, revisited the same topics and terms that were legislated in DOMA and IIRAIRA. Therefore, their defeat was less about the change in our political climate, and more about the redundancy of the legislation. However, it is because these pieces of legislation were written and approved all the way to the Senate, even though they mostly state the same regulations set forth ten years earlier, that makes them so meaningful.

Now, I am not asserting that these two pieces of legislation were exactly the same as DOMA and IIRAIRA. In fact, in many ways these pieces were far more dangerous. The FMA was an attempt to change the U.S. Constitution and define marriage between a man and a woman once and for all, and H.R. 4437 attempted to make undocumented immigrants felons based solely on the status of their lack of documentation. Because these bills were both seen as extreme measures, the argument could be made that they disrupted the notion of tolerance and multiculturalism that most Americans believe we epitomize. However, the public discourse surrounding the bills was not tolerant at all, and the ways that the brand of the heteronormative U.S. family circulated were quite similar to the discussions from ten years earlier.

The timing of these initiatives is important to note. In 2006, we were three years into a war on foreign soil that has no apparent end and was in response to one of the most damaging attacks to our nation; we were twelve years into the neoliberal trade agreements of NAFTA and CAFTA and reaping the benefits of job loss, pollution, and depletion of national resources across the globe, and were (and perhaps still are) in the wake of some of the most conservative legislation being proposed throughout the country (states banning same sex marriage; English-only initiatives; banning illegal immigrants from townships). There was an urgency in U.S. politics to keep the American people safe. But how could that be done when so many of our resources were being sent out into that world? This contradiction had to be faced, and what better way than to assert a definitive standard about who belongs, who does not, and who deserves protection by employing the brand of the family.

The most obvious example of using the family to define the nation was in the Federal Marriage Act (FMA) that was going to once and for all name marriage as a heterosexual enterprise in the United States. The second clause was short and sweet, and its language clearly stated its intention to limit what individual states could call "marriage" by nationally defining the term with no uncertainty. The FMA reads as follows:

> Marriage in the United States shall consist of the union of a man and a woman. Neither this Constitution, nor the constitution of any State, shall be construed to require that marriage or the legal incidents thereof be conferred upon other than the union of a man and a woman. (FMA sec. 2)

Instead of using the term "spouse," as did DOMA, which focuses on the individuals who are a part of the union, this piece of legislation works to define the institution of marriage itself. This move to define the larger institution, instead of the members therein, shows just how important the institution as a whole has become. The movement from spouse to marriage is seemingly a jump in scale from the intimate to the juridical, from the individual to the communal.

Changing the definition from the intimate couplings of marriage to the institution itself resonates with the newfound anxiety about neoliberal movements of bodies and capital through the United States. It makes sense that there needs to be greater control over our definitions of ourselves and the state when that state is continually shifting its boundaries in the name of terror and/or capital.

The rhetoric of the war on terror is an important piece here, as well. From September 11, 2001, the official rhetoric in the U.S. media and from our leaders in government has been about terror. There are many things that we should fear, and most of these are threats that will enter our homes and tear apart our most intimate relationships. From the coverage of those who lost their lives in the Twin Towers and the over-emphasis on the ways in which the government and media were protecting their families to the constant reminder on every major media station of the level of the terror alert, the media and government have established the status quo of American life as one of fear and the need for protection.

The year 2006, then, was a different moment than 1996, and it created a different kind of context for those who are protecting the family. Yes, in 1996 there was vehement discussion surrounding issues of immigration and same-sex marriage, and in 1996 the legislation satisfied most who wanted reforms without changing the Constitution or naming immigrants felons. But this was before September 11th and its surrounding rhetoric established a constant feeling of anxiety among Americans. When the rhetoric of fear is coupled with discussions of the national debt, a trillion-dollar war, and white-collar job outsourcing, Americans were left to feel that fear and anxiety very acutely. Therefore, the rhetoric surrounding the FMA and H.R. 4437 was more intense and more urgent.

An example of this kind of urgency could be found in the comments made by Sen. Sam Brownback (R-KA) that were published in newspapers throughout the United States. His comments were made in light of FMA's defeat, but according to Brownback, the war was far from over. He states: "We're making progress, and we're not going to stop until marriage between a man and a woman is protected . . . protected in the courts, protected in the Constitution, but most of all, protected for the people and for the future of our children in this society." Sen. Brownback's comments, although obviously cheap politicking, still reveal how the brand of protection is central in these debates. In one short statement, Brownback says "protected" four times. This reveals that the FMA's goal was to protect the American family from those who would cause it harm—in this case, gays and lesbians. Brownback is a right-wing Christian conservative, so his rhetoric will obviously be more forceful than those who are moderate on this issue. However, this comment, taken along with the results of the 2004 election (in which eleven states banned same-sex marriage within their jurisdiction), shows the ways in which post–9/11 America clearly feels the need to protect the family from threats both internal and external.

Again, what is important to note here is that, even though two years prior several states banned same-sex marriage, and ten years prior the term "spouse" was defined as a person of the opposite sex, there was still a perceived need to settle this question by changing the U.S. Constitution. This need is related to the need to label particular immigrants felons, not because they have committed a violent crime, but rather because they are in violation of immigration rules and status. Both of these groups, gays and lesbians and undocumented immigrants, pose a direct threat to the post–9/11 definition of "citizen" and what it means to be an American. This move to criminalize those who are different and/or threatening is the same move made in H.R. 4437. Even though the legislation has the same clause about domestic violence as IIRAIRA, H.R. 4437, much like FMA, broadens the scope of the legislation to establish regulation and define threats inside particular communities. What is striking, however, is the way in which the discourse surrounding the community echoes the discourse surrounding the family in the domestic violence clauses.

An example of this is found in section 602 "Detention of the Alien," subsection 4 "Conditions for Extensions," wherein the legislation discusses the possible reasons to detain an alien, which may or may not be related to his initial cause of arrest. Section iii and iv work together to define an alien as a particular threat to a community, but the language that is used is reminiscent of the language in the domestic violence clause, which allows for immediate deportation and/or arrest of an alien. The two sections read as follows:

> (iii) Based on information available to the Secretary (including information from the intelligence community, and without regard to grounds upon which the alien was ordered removed), there is reason to believe that the release of the alien would threaten the national security of the United States.
>
> (iv) The release of the alien will threaten the safety of the community or any person, the conditions of release cannot reasonably be expected to insure the safety of the community or any person. (Sec 602, 4, iii and iv)

The discussion of threats to the safety of an individual, community, and the nation itself is much the same characterization of the potential threat that is posed to a family by an alien who has perpetrated domestic violence. Again we see the mobilization of threats, but instead of focusing the attacks on the family, as it did in IIRAIRA, this rhetoric is now applied to the larger relationship structures of community and nation. Although the family is not present in this discussion, these narratives of protection are formed on rhetorical patterns of protection that were established around the family unit.

It is the belief in a threat and the need to insure the safety of the community that calls to mind the rhetoric of the domestic violence clause, and it also mirrors the media discourse surrounding the FMA. We are reminded that these alien detainees *did* commit some crime, and that is why they are in custody in the first place. The parenthetical in section iii reminds us of this, and even if that is not the reason for the continued detention, there was an initial crime that was committed to get them into custody. So these aliens are doubly dangerous. They are not only criminals, or illegal, they are also now a threat to our nations, communities, and individuals.

No longer are we merely talking about threats to a specific household. Instead, we are speaking of threats to the community and the nation, as well as individuals who may or may not be in our family. This move serves not only to denote the new found anxiety and fear that has permeated state and media rhetoric post–9/11, but it also alludes to the ways in which the family, community, and the nation represent a metonymic chain. The relationships between those in communities and even the nation become personal and intimate through the rhetoric of threat and protection, and when paralleled with the rhetoric of marriage and family proposed in the FMA, we can begin to see that these radically different scales of relationships are equated in their rhetorical production.

It makes sense, then, that the media discussion around H.R. 4437 primarily used the image of the immigrant as upstanding family member, or connected to other U.S. citizens through filial relationships. The legitimizing brand of the family cannot be denied, and it becomes imperative to argue within the discourses provided to make particular othered experience visible. Immigrants cannot claim connection through nationhood because often they are perceived as non-citizens or less than citizens, and it is difficult for them to find connection in terms of community because they are so often ostracized from the U.S. community at large. Therefore, as a point of connection, the use of the family member with ties to U.S. citizenship through that affiliation seems to be the easiest way to articulate their position as one that is familiar and non-threatening.

However, this also serves to mask the greater material issues that arise when the intensity of the legislation and the rhetoric surrounding it rises. The intensity of the counter-discourse, as well as the adherence to appropriate narratives of family, also rises. This can be seen in the media coverage of H.R. 4437. The presence of the family is more real and more aggressive than the stories we see in 1996. The term "family unity" is a rallying cry for activists across the country, and even moderate politicians are granting the importance of familial relationships in their opposition to the bill. So then the rhetorical purpose of the brand of the family is to mask the global flows of money and governmentality by creating the notion of a national family or core national values—all the while exporting jobs, military, and money. Therefore, it is not merely the move to the family as a talking point, but it is a move to the family as the primary unit of political discourse that is of note.

THE INTENSITY OF PROTECTION: THE MOVE TOWARD ASSEMBLING BRANDED THREATS

The interweaving of who can be a family, who cannot, and how those definitions helped the state identify as a nation in 1996, are, in 2006, becoming the means of self-identification as a member of the state as well. The shift to the reciprocal nature of state legitimation makes sense in the context of the new heightened anxiety and sense of urgency surrounding definitions of national identity and safety. It is not enough to be in the nation; now one has to believe as the nation believes to prove that they really belong. It is not enough to merely follow the legal rules for citizenship; now one has to exemplify what it means to be an American by being part of a family. And as we have seen, there is only one particular kind of family that will create citizens—one that is white and heterosexual. If one does not fit that definition, one is a threat that is feared and used to fuel the anxiety surrounding the decline of the nation, or of civilization as we know it.

These fears can be seen in the rhetoric of our politicians, news leaders, and independent presses throughout the United States. A good example of this is Frank Rich's op-ed piece, "How the Hispanics became Homosexuals," in the *New York Times*. He quotes both a Fox News anchor as well as a congressional candidate to show the ways in which the attacks on immigrants and gays and lesbians work together to provide a picture of a protectionist America that is in the throes of its own decline-of-civilization narrative. Rich states:

> "What a repellent spectacle," the Fox News anchor Brit Hume said when surveying masses of immigrant demonstrators, some of them waving Mexican flags, in April. Hearing of a Spanish version of "The Star-Spangled Banner," Lamar Alexander, a Republican from Tennessee, introduced a Senate resolution calling for the national anthem to be sung only in English. There was no more point to that gratuitous bit of grandstanding than there was to the D.O.A. marriage amendment. Or more accurately, both had the same point: stirring up animosity against a group that can be branded an enemy of civilization as we know it.
> Vernon Robinson, a Republican Congressional candidate challenging the Democratic incumbent Brad Miller in North Carolina, has run an ad warning that "if Miller had his way, America would be nothing but one big fiesta for illegal aliens and homosexuals."

The pervasiveness of the protection of the family and the identification and expulsion of potential threats from the realm of citizenship has reached the level of spectacle[16]—a spectacle whose intensity creates a material need for those ostracized from the realm of citizenship and the nation to prove themselves worthy on the state's terms. Those who do not fit into those categories are suspect at best and a threat at worst. These bodies not only reinforce the need for protection for the national family, but they also define the limits of the national family by establishing who belongs and who does not.

It is not a stretch, then, to speak of the nation as a family that must be protected by the laws it establishes. And those laws must be all-encompassing to protect families from threats both visible and invisible. As we move more toward spectacle, we become further removed from the branding of consumer (or material) protection, and more deeply embedded in the branding of protection—the rhetoric which animates discussions of family at the national level. Often these narratives of protection attempt to combine discussions of protection and morality by positing others who serve to disturb national order through their very contact with the family. But as 9/11 showed us, the family is not the only group in jeopardy. The nation is also under attack from the outside. Therefore, to make the nation strong, we must attempt to stop the attacks from the inside by clearly defining who we are, by articulating who we are not. Because the family is what makes our nation strong, it is the family unit that is used to define who we are and who we are not in times of economic and political uncertainty. It is through enforcement and definition of threats through the use of affective intensity that the branding of protection can be implemented. And the more pervasive the threat, the more stringent the laws must become. And the more stringent the laws, the more intense the brands must become.

NOTES

1. Lee Edelman posits children as the central figure of the U.S. nation-state. He claims that the queer male presents the greatest threat to the structures of oppression. They disrupt procreation and are not seen as "life-givers," like heterosexual men.

2. Lisa Duggan critiques Lee Edelman's *No Future* as universalist in its construction of children. She sees his forwarding of the centrality of the "unencumbered child" as a 1950s U.S. development that has changed over the past sixty years because of divorce rates, economic downturns, and declines in government spending. Therefore the myth of family/nation=children is just a myth; or, as I am arguing, a brand.

3. Keillor says nothing about the statistic that 80 percent of violence against women and children happens in the home. In other words, the fantasy of a traditional, safe, home space has always been just that—a fantasy.

4. Chandan Reddy discusses "the family" as a discursive and political feature central to neoliberalism. He claims it allows certain groups (white, middle class, heterosexual) to become quintessential subjects of the nation-state. Yet, he is quick to demonstrate how other groups (non-white, immigrant, GLBT bodies) are devalued and marked as surplus (both emotionally and economically). And it is through the disenfranchisement of those bodies that capital keeps circulating.

5. In "On Governmentality" Foucault asserts that as far back as the eighteenth century the family became the central focus of governmental policy. It was the need to

protect the nation, as represented by individual families that created new forms of surveillance and policing by the state. He states: "The family becomes an instrument rather than a model: the privileged instrument for the government of the population and not the chimerical model for good government: this shift from the level of the model to that of the instrument is, I believe, absolutely fundamental, and it is from the middle of the 18th century that the family appears in this dimension of instrumentality with respect to the population: hence the campaigns on morality, marriage vaccinations, etc" (17). These state practices focusing on protecting the family also serve, however, to place the family at the center of government. The state is a collective of families, and it is assumed that all of those families have similar needs and desires that must be regulated by the state. Therefore, the nation takes on the identity of the über-family, a synecdochic representation—the whole taking the place of all of the parts.

6. The more sensational term for the rise of supply-side economics.

7. Thomas Frank's *What's the Matter with Kansas?* analyzes the economic conditions and voting records of the state of Kansas. He reveals that the citizens of the state often vote against more liberal measures that would better their economic conditions. He claims that they vote against their own self-interest because of a commitment to conservative family values, and that these discourses allow working class citizens to remain powerful in times of economic downturn.

8. It can be argued that this continues throughout political elections even today. The sexual indiscretions of John Edwards and numerous other Republican senators have ended their political careers. It matters not whether they are good politicians, serve their constituencies, but instead, their value as a public official is judged on how well they practice monogamy.

9. The heterosexual family works as a means to normativize the behavior of the citizenry. This is an important step because if we are to assume that a democracy is made up of its citizens, then whatever the normal behavior of those citizens is will help to define the state. In other words, creating a narrative of a mixed-gendered family, whether in the name of ironic nostalgia or not, functions to help the nation rebuild itself and reaffirm its identity.

10. As Brian Massumi argues in *Parables for the Virtual: Movement, Affect, Sensation,* the event of image reception takes place on several levels: there is a level of intensity and a level of qualification. Therefore, unlike Kenneth Burke and even Wendy Hesford who posit affective identification within contexts and situations of rhetorical practice, Massumi sees intensities as circulating prior to any spoken words. Affective intensities create relationships between bodies before rhetorical situations and events present themselves, and without these visceral and virtual happenings, affective identification would not be as effective.

11. Once again, the law implies certain assumptions of Americanness by implementing limited options and possibilities for legal immigrants to continue their stay in the United States because of issues of language, money, and access to services.

12. In *Strange Encounters*, Sara Ahmed discusses the ways in which law and culture (from film to neighborhood watch) work together to define a set of acceptable others and non-acceptable others. The acceptable others are used to make the citizens of the nation feel benevolent and secure in their multicultural identities. The other non-acceptable others, then, are marked as dangerous and unintelligible. They must, therefore, be expelled from the nation-state in order to help define who the citizens (and thus the nation) are not.

13. M. Jacqui Alexander discusses the appropriation of feminist discourse in order to re-inscribe primogenitor, patriarchal rule in the home, as well as to establish clearly defined private property laws in marriage through domestic violence legislation. She shows the ways in which the legislation in the Bahamas prescribed a particular set of conditions and practices surrounding domestic violence that only allowed for claims to be made from within a marital home with appropriate documentation. Even though these laws seemed to be enacted because of feminist activist agitation, the laws actually served to reestablish patriarchal rule by directly connecting the notions of home and

family to property ownership by introducing the terms mortgage and mortgager into the legislation. Although the U.S. law reads very differently than the law ratified in the Bahamas, it still draws from some of these same histories of marriage as a financial institution where women and children were property of the husband/father, much like the homes they inhabited. The appearance of the terms "spouse" and "household" allude to these connections, even though they are not stated directly.

14. I take this term from Judith Butler, who, in her article "Is Kinship Always Already Heterosexual?" discusses the need for GLBT couples to seek legitimation from the state not only for the rights it affords, but also for the psychic well-being recognition brings. Thus legitimation is not only a material term, but also an affective one, as well.

15. The Full Faith and Credit Clause is an attempt to protect states' rights by asserting that as citizens move between states the legal contracts they enter into in one state (such as marriage, civil unions, and property ownership) will be recognized in another state. This is a means of preserving the republic as a confederation of states with local authority that are joined by way of federal recognition of that authority. It is the most compelling argument against laws like DOMA.

16. Spectacle refers to Guy Debord's *Society of the Spectacle*, in which he discusses how postmodern culture has become so constructed that it has attained the level of spectacle even in everyday life.

THREE

(Dis)Embodying the Branding of Protection

Assemblage in the ICE Age

THE RIGHT TO ASSEMBLAGE: LAURA'S PHONE CALL

At the end of chapter two, I described the shift from the branding of protection to the branding of terror after the September 11, 2001, attacks on the United States. In this chapter, that shift will be discussed as a change in the rhetorical practice of branding. No longer were the solitary brands of "immigrant," "GLBT person," or "family" powerful enough to affectively stimulate the cultural imaginary of the United States. Instead, the brands of "terror" and "predator" become those from which the U.S. citizenry must seek protection. These brands, at their base, still function as a means to evacuate the materiality of bodies and deliver a simple affective narrative of national wholeness. But how the brands are constructed and mobilized has changed.

Instead of singular brands, brands are now assembled under larger branded terms, such as "threat," "terror," and "homeland." These all-encompassing brands still do not materialize the economic or political consequences of the bodies which inhabit or inspire them. Instead, they draw together the ideological histories of each brand as a means to create a totalizing and ever present set of threats. In other words, when brands are assembled the process allows for an exchange of characteristics without any causal, analogous, or material correspondence. What is created, then, is an über-threat against which protection becomes almost impossible. Therefore, as a nation, we must become vigilant in our efforts to protect our "homeland."

This chapter seeks to articulate the complex process of rhetorical assemblage by demonstrating how brands, when assembled, create totalizing, but at the same time amorphous, threats. Additionally, it will demonstrate that these assembled brands are then used to solidify the nation-state's move toward neoliberal governmentality. That is, they allow the nation-state to reclaim its right to police its national citizenry both at home and abroad. This may seem at odds with the Deleuzian society of control that I described in chapter one. However, it is my contention that the neoliberal U.S. nation-state, post–9/11, is attempting to reassert its identity as a whole nation all the while diversifying its political, economic, and militaristic ambitions. In other words, the United States's investment in its own national identity is equally as precarious as that of its citizens. After the attacks of September 11, 2001, it was not enough for the nation-state to be affectively whole, they needed to be materially whole as well.

The United States did not want to limit its economic or political diversification or its deep commitment to neoliberalism. However, it did want to reify its national identity by establishing itself once again as a strong military presence at home and abroad. Therefore, it is not surprising that after a large-scale domestic attack, the nation-state would attempt to regulate its own body politic through the policing of terror at home and abroad. So instead of merely using brands to do the ideological and rhetorical work of nation building, as described in chapter two, the United States began to assemble brands to heighten the terror of its citizens at home and abroad. When that terror was heightened, they began to assemble working agencies to police those threats. This chapter, then, discusses how even though brands may not hold materiality themselves, they can have vast material consequences for not only those who are branded, but for entire nation-states as well.

The development of Immigration and Customs Enforcement (ICE), which I will discuss at length in this chapter, is one of those material consequences. But it is not branding alone that brought about the development of ICE. Instead, it was the assembling of vastly different brands into a single narrative of threat, one that had to be policed by a single group of specialists. No longer were immigrants, sexual predators, or computer hackers seen as different criminals. Under ICE, they were housed together due to the possibility of crossover in criminal activity, no matter how materially limited that possibility may be. By assembling criminals through the material policing of their bodies and the branding of their crimes, ICE has developed an evolving threat matrix where anyone can move from a misdemeanor to a felon in one step.

Therein lies the danger of assembling brands. Rhetorical assemblage serves to link together identifiable figures with, as Duggan claims, very specific racial, gendered, and sexualized histories. Those histories and cultural assumptions are then drawn together to create a larger set of threats. The presence of identifiable branded identities is not a contradiction within the logic of the assemblage. In fact, as Puar has noted, the assemblage needs the deep history and context of these identifiable brands to fuel its associations. Without these seemingly well-defined historical identities, the assemblage could not function as seamlessly as it does. In other words, the assemblage needs the historical markings which are carried on the brands to create intense threats through association.

These assembled brands of pervasive global threat have entered the national imaginary, and we can see the brands discussed in chapter two employed as parts of these über-brands. For example, on December 8, 2006, the Los Angeles chapter of Solidarity.org, a pro-immigrant rights group, received a hateful voice mail message. It was from a woman who was later discovered to be from the Arizona chapter of the anti-immigrant group gainusa.org. The woman who identified herself in subsequent emails to the group as "Laura," attempted to challenge the rhetoric of the immigrant rights movement by reiterating that those who enter the United States without appropriate papers are in fact "illegal aliens" and not immigrants of any kind. She states:

> You are not immigrants. You are illegal aliens. That is the correct immigration term for sneaks, cheats, and liars. People who sneak into our country; spit on our laws; steal our peoples' identification. That's what you are. You are criminals. Immigrants apply to come to this country. Then they comply with all kinds of requirements like background checks and health checks. And then they get on line and they wait like human beings. Not like crud cheats and liars like illegal aliens. [pause] You will be deported. Stop manipulating our words. Stop trying to manipulate our people. If we go to your country you know that that is a felony. In Mexico it's a felony. And in most other countries it's a felony. Stop trying to take advantage of our laws. Murderers are human beings also, but they're still murderers. Rapists and thieves are still are [sic] human beings, but they are still rapists and thieves. And you people are illegal aliens [hang up]. ("Laura" 12/8/06)

There are several things of note in "Laura's" statement. First, Laura recognizes the rhetoric of the immigrant rights movement and their use of the term "undocumented immigrants" instead of "illegal aliens." This is an important move in the rhetorical construction ot who is crossing the border and how U.S. citizens can begin to think of them. By using the term undocumented instead of illegal and immigrant instead of alien, the immigrant rights movement is attempting to shift the immigration debate from one centered on felonious actions (illegal) by unidentifiable people (aliens) to one of the bureaucratic status (undocumented) of a definable group of people (immigrants). But for "Laura," that rhetorical move is one of manipulation. What is evident from "Laura's" comment and its intended audience is that the immigration debate is one where language and word choice are critical components for both sides of the debate.

But "Laura's" comment also reveals some key assumptions about who immigrates into our country and what they are *really* doing here. First of all, according to "Laura" these people are "sneaks, cheats, and liars" who "sneak into our country; spit on our laws; and steal our peoples' identification"—much as "murderers, rapists, and thieves," "illegal aliens" may be human beings, but ultimately they are defined as "illegal aliens." By including multiple types of criminals together—thieves, murderers, sexual predators, and illegal immigrants—who do not really have anything to do with one another, Laura is creating an *assemblage of threat*; whose characteristics are then attached to "illegal aliens." Her move to compile different criminal identities, and then associate those characteristics with one particular type of criminal is a move, which I will discuss at length later in this chapter, toward assemblage—wherein the characteristics of figures are removed from the original identities associated with the figures and combined to create an all pervasive or über-threatening criminal.

"Laura's" message demonstrates, however crudely, the ways in which assemblage operates by creating associations of threats through the mere mention, no matter how faulty the connection, between these identities.[1] Part of the work of the assemblage is to demonstrate how the threat in question, in this case the "illegal alien," is not only dangerous because of its own associations, but is far more dangerous because of its association with other more violent criminals. Therefore, an assemblage is a means with which to heighten the affective intensity surrounding the discussions of threat, and "Laura's" statement works to do just that. "Laura" is showing the severity of the threat posed to the United States by undocumented immigrants. This echoes her earlier sentiments that "illegal immigrants" are "sneaks, cheats, and liars"—all characteristics of successful thievery—and that there are documented cases of the severity of their crime—identity theft of presumably law abiding citizens.

"Laura's" accusation of thievery, however, is not centered on the notion that "illegal immigrants" actually steal anything, although there is an implicit connection to the idea that not "getting on line" is in some way a stealing of a privilege that is not theirs to take. Instead, their crime is based solely on their immigration status. "Laura" invokes Mexico's immigration law to support her claim, and discusses how even though H.R. 4437, as discussed in chapter two, may not have passed, "illegal immigrants" are felons, and they (the illegal immigrants) should know this because their presumed home country has the same law. The connection "Laura" makes to Mexican immigration policy functions not only to show how the United States is a more benevolent country than Mexico—because we do have legal paths to citizenship—but to also show that those entering this country should not expect special treatment because they would not be extended the same in their own country.

Additionally, this move to link immigrants to Mexico reveals an assumption that "illegal immigrants" come from Mexico. "Laura's" statement does not only criminalize "illegal immigrants" but links them directly with a specific national population. This move racializes the immigration debate, and even though "Laura" never specifically calls "illegal immigrants" Mexicans, her nod to Mexican immigration law prefaced by "if we go to *your* country" (emphasis mine) makes a clear case that for "Laura" the "illegal immigrant" problem in this country is coming from a specific place (Mexico) and can be attributed to a specific population (Mexicans). For "Laura," not only are undocumented immigrants felons, but they are Mexican, as well. Even when the rhetoric does not specifically link the two, much like "Laura's" rhetoric it creates associations through contiguity—naming legal immigrants in the same paragraph as particular countries, naming illegal immigrants criminals by printing information about thieves and rapists in the same paragraph.

As I have discussed throughout both chapters one and two, media and governmental rhetorical outlets have made immigrant and GLBT bodies into brands. But these brands do not serve as markers of particular lifestyles to emulate the way traditional corporate brands do. Instead, they serve as cautionary tales of what to avoid, who to fear, and who is outside the norm of citizenship. Because of the shift to neoliberal governmentality wherein the state no longer cares for its citizens as it did under liberal governmentality, branding serves to create a population whose sole purpose is to work for capital, instead of being accepted into the nation-state as citizens. These bodies, then, are made into brands and are evacuated of any human characteristics. Thus they are turned into objects from which citizens need protection. "Laura's" rhetoric also demonstrates how post–9/11 figures are functioning differently, all the while drawing on the traces of previous historical usages. Furthermore, with the collapsing of government infrastructure post–9/11 and the development of über-security forces such as the Immigration and Customs Enforcement Agency (ICE), these brands are placed together under the same umbrella of surveillance; thus, the qualities of brands become applied to another through proximity, not through causality, analogy, or logic.

Within post–9/11 neoliberal logic(s), clearly identifiable threats are no longer the norm. Instead, the rhetoric surrounding protection and threat works to create an ever present, unidentifiable, yet strangely familiar, series of threats. The discussion of these threats uses affective identification, as discussed in chapter one, to help citizens recognize just how much they need protection. The shift toward assemblage—creating multivalanced threat through contiguity, much as "Laura" does—creates the branding of terror. These threats create new circumstances for law enforcement which impacts citizens and non-citizens alike. This chapter discusses the presence of assemblage within this moment and the ways in which it impacts how brands circulate.

Like "Laura's" phone call, post–9/11 rhetorics of terror create the need for new mobilizations of brands through the notion of the assemblage (the terrorist, the predator). The assemblage works to produce contradictory identities and affective figures that are both mobilized in the name of governmental threat and protection. Puar, as discussed in chapter one, argues that rhetoric is not only used to produce intensities, but it is used interchangeably to create an assemblage of threat that requires totalizing governmental and occasionally coercive means of protection.

ASSEMBLING THE "WAR ON TERROR": POST-9/11'S BRANDING OF TERROR

The "war on terror" has been defined since September 11, 2001, as a state of ever-present non-visible threat, which creates uncertainty, fear, and uneasiness within the body politic. The rhetoric of terror and the branding of threats therein create a need for citizens to be always aware of what cannot be identified or seen. In fact, this rhetoric creates a notion of a citizen who functions not only as a consumer of media, goods, and ideology, but also a citizen who consumes information about who and what they should be vigilant against. This knowledge in turn allows them to become actively involved in surveillance of the nation, their property, and each other. This implicitly expands the logic of personal responsibility into the realm of security and protection. Therefore, the branding of terror not only redefines who or what is a threat to the nation, but also helps to redefine who qualifies as a citizen and as such what a citizen must do for the nation.

President George W. Bush, in his speech four days after the World Trade Center attacks, made it very clear that the "enemy" is not one that can be "seen," but instead, is an enemy that we will have to reveal. He states:

> This is a conflict without battlefields or beachheads, a conflict with opponents who believe they are invisible. Yet, they are mistaken. They will be exposed, and they will discover what others in the past have learned: Those who make war against the United States have chosen their own destruction. (Bush 9/15/2001)

The presence of invisibility and the need that it creates to expose the enemy is important to note. It is no longer possible to point to a country, an ethnicity, or a well-defined group to find danger. Yet, as discussed in chapter two, the nature of neoliberal logics means that these invisible threats are always already raced, classed, and gendered in particular ways. So even though assembling brands creates the illusion of an amorphous, non-identifiable, ever-present threat, the threats are still intelligible and affective because of their cultural and historical constructions.

The branding of terror not only changes who is threatening the United States, but it also changes the very nature of war. War is no longer being fought as an isolated event, but it too is now an invisible and ever-present threat. Therefore all citizens of the United States must be aware that there are invisible enemies who are waging invisible wars against us who must be stopped, even though we cannot see them. Danger must be discovered, and it is possible that it is in places where we might not even conceive of it. Nevertheless, one thing is certain; the United States and its individual citizens will expose this danger and insure that it is brought to justice.

This ever-pervasive threat is branded "the terrorist." Terrorists are both individuals and members of groups, both identifiable by their deeds and anomalous in their nature, and both visible and invisible at once. Jasbir Puar and Amit Rai, in their analysis of post–9/11 terrorist images, discuss the ways in which the terrorist is produced as an assemblage of many traits that are at once tied to particular social groups *and* removed from those bodies and presented as behaviors and/or traits. For Puar and Rai, these moves create new ways of understanding representation and identity within the context of patriotism in a post–9/11 world.

Puar and Rai discuss how the figure of the terrorist represents not only our national anxieties about terror, but also reveals our basic fears of figures we do not know and cannot readily see and/or understand. They use the theoretical example of the Foucauldian monster to explain the ways in which the terrorist represents a grotesque figure that must either be redeemed or contained. The monster is a figure that exists at the limits of intelligibility, making it both visible and invisible at once. Puar and Rai explain:

> "What links the monster-terrorist to the figure of the individual to be corrected is first and foremost the racialized and deviant psyche. . . . It is the figure of the inexplicable that continues to haunt civilization grids that the Western war machine would deploy in its attempt to 'understand the terrorist psyche'" ("Monster, Terrorist, Fag" 125).

The uncanny, the inexplicable, the (in)visible is central to the branding of terror, and in order to "fight" what we cannot see, terrorism studies have attempted to understand particular psychological markers of "the terrorist" in order to make the terrorist more knowable, and thus redeemable.

If the terrorist becomes knowable, it becomes an other, as discussed in chapter one, who we can absorb into the nation-state, thus helping us to establish the national citizenry as generous and also non-terrorist. But the assemblage of the terrorist-monster resists classification, and therefore, changes how threat and protection are understood. No longer is the terrorist a member of an easily identifiable group or psychological type.

Instead it is unknowable, unreadable, and in that sense unreachable within our modernist frameworks of identity. By tracing these shifts, we can begin to see the ways in which the rhetoric surrounding threat and terror is always in motion—mobilizing new dangerous assemblages and reassemblages.

The branding of terror, based on the assemblage of the terrorist, which Puar and Rai discuss, is seen working throughout the Presidential addresses given directly following 9/11 and commemorating the passage of the Patriot Act. Bush in his address to the nation in November 2001 described the new duties of a citizen as linked to the policing of terrorists. This address was made merely two months after the events of September 11th, and it was an attempt to reassure U.S. citizens that they did not need to rely only on the government for protection from "evil," but they could also rely on one another. What is important to note about the context of this speech is that it commemorates the passing of the Patriot Act, a piece of national legislation that limits individual rights in the name of national security. But the Patriot Act, and its legal precedents, is barely mentioned in the text. Instead of discussing the significant changes to the rights of citizens, the responsibilities of citizens are articulated. This speech, then, invokes and extends the neoliberal logic of personal responsibility at work in the United States since the early 1980s. Bush stated:

> Our citizens have new responsibilities. We must be vigilant. Obviously, we must inspect our mail, and stay informed on public health matters. We will not give in to exaggerated fears or passing rumors. We will rely on good judgment and good, old common sense. We will care for those who have lost loved ones, and comfort those who might at times feel afraid. We will not judge fellow Americans by appearance, ethnic background, or religious faith. We will defend the values of country, and we will live by them. We will persevere in this struggle, no matter how long it takes to prevail. (Bush 11/8/2001)

The Patriot Act limits many rights that have been seen by critics of the act as central to liberal governance—something which the United States has historically sworn to protect. But instead of focusing on the loss of rights, Bush discusses the ways in which citizens need to behave to fulfill the promise of America. His focus on vigilance, good judgment and compassion seems fairly innocuous, but it is setting the terms of citizenship post–9/11. It is defining citizenship as a list of actions, rather than judging it on "appearance, ethnic background, or religious faith." Additionally, it extends the logic of personal responsibility from one's own private property and family to the needs of the nation as a whole. Therefore, American-ness, much like what is dangerous, is not visible. Instead, it must be revealed through action and distinguished by behavior. Because you cannot tell by sight who is a threat, Americans must be vigilant not only to protect themselves from these invisible threats, but also to prove that they themselves are not a threat.

This shift to the invisible threat that cannot be known or understood by our Western knowledge base creates not only a new enemy, but also a new citizen who must be wary of impending threat at all times. It is the redefinition of citizenship through the redefinition of terrorism that is critical in our post–9/11 world. It is not enough to read the terrorist as invisible and unknowable. Rather, we must begin to see the connection between the identification of that unknowability and the legal definitions of citizenship and patriotism. Puar and Rai state: "In the name of patriotism, a double-framed reality and a double movement of power tie together the production of docile patriots. . . . Such monsters, through their very example, provide patriotism with its own pedagogies of normalization" (136). For Puar and Rai the bodies of monsters allow us to enact new forms of patriotism that are tied to notions of citizenship.[2] Both Bush's speeches and the Patriot Act present the new responsibilities citizens must abide in the name of patriotism, and those responsibilities often allow for the establishment of an internal policing that mirrors the collapse of legal jurisdiction that is happening in the name of protection of the national family.

The turn toward individual responsible behavior and policing is not only present in presidential rhetoric post–9/11. Even the Patriot Act establishes who deserves protection and who we need to be protected against by clearly labeling behaviors that are considered terrorist actions. Furthermore, the Patriot Act establishes the need to ensure the rights (no matter how limited they may be at this point) of *all* American citizens, and it is sure to establish early in the legislation how citizenship is not determined by race, ethnic, or religious affiliation. Instead, Americanness is based on citizenship and as such must be protected. It states:

> (b) Sense of Congress.—It is the sense of Congress that—
> (1) the civil rights and civil liberties of all Americans, including Arab Americans, Muslim Americans, and Americans from South Asia, must be protected, and that every effort must be taken to preserve their safety;
> (2) any acts of violence or discrimination against any Americans be condemned; and
> (3) the Nation is called upon to recognize the patriotism of fellow citizens from all ethnic, racial, and religious backgrounds. (Sec. 102 b1-3)

The Sense of Congress appears in the first section of the legislation, and its primacy is important to note for a couple of reasons. First, its presence in the beginning of the legislation that is primarily aimed at defining and defending against terror is a way for the United States to acknowledge that terrorism is not associated with one social group. Therefore, the United States recognizes that it must take every precaution to put an end to the discrimination or branded associations made between Arab, Muslim, and South East Asian bodies.

Furthermore, by acknowledging the presence of this kind of racial profiling and discrimination at the beginning of the document that will attempt to define what makes a terrorist and what citizens can do to act against them, it is removing the figure of terrorist from particular bodies and reaffirming that terror is an invisible threat defined by action rather than racial, ethnic, religious, or group affiliation. But by creating an assemblage, the rhetoric of threat reattaches the new formations of threat onto particular bodies, and as such the categories of identity become flexible, fluid, and even harder to decipher. In other words, through the assemblage, Congress can both recognize the racialization of the terrorist figure and also reveal the ways in which said figure cannot be fully identified by race alone. Congress, through the use of the assemblage, is asserting the invisibility of terror, and thus creating a need for new responsibilities, limited rights, and vigilance from all citizens.

This disclaimer allows the United States to present itself as aware and compassionate, one of the traits of citizenship according to Bush. This move to recognize that citizens are not determined by their appearance but by their deeds is critical in a time when citizenship is burdened with new responsibilities because of the privileging of *personal responsibility* and privatization. As discussed in chapter one, these parallel neoliberal logics create a citizenry that must take care of themselves financially and morally, all the while being stripped of their state mandated rights. The U.S. nation-state, then, appears to be more a representation of all of its citizens than a governing body, and as such, it is presented as compassionate, aware, and vigilant in the fight against terror at home and abroad. Again, the presence of the final clause about all citizens, no matter their backgrounds or affiliations, needing to be judged by their patriotism creates a new legal definition of what it means to be a citizen. Now, not only are citizens defined by official discourses; they are also created through their patriotic acts. In this way, anyone can be a citizen, even those who may look like the terrorists responsible for 9/11.

The need to create a national identity that is posited on protection from terror is stated in the name of the Patriot Act itself. The full name of the act is "Uniting and Strengthening America by Providing Appropriate Tools Required to Intercept and Obstruct Terrorism (USA Patriot) Act of 2001." The title explains just what the Patriot Act is supposed to do. It is supposed to give the United States a strong unified identity by providing the means and methods (the tools) to learn of (intercept) and stop (obstruct) terrorism. In other words, this act is defining the strength of the United States in terms of how well it defends itself against terror; through this defense the United States will become unified, thus strong. Although that last sentence presents a tautology, the logic behind the Patriot Act is in fact tautological. It is an act that is supposed to create a strength and unity on the knowledge and defense of terror. Therefore, by defending itself, the nation becomes strong and unified. In other words, the function of the Patriot Act and the national speeches surrounding it is to create an environment in which the nation is in need of protection, and the only way it can become strong is to protect itself through the vigilance of the government and its citizenry.

ASSEMBLING PROTECTION: THE DEVELOPMENT OF ICE

This assemblage model is not only present in the rhetoric of the legislation and media right after 9/11. It is also materially apparent in the ways brands have been mobilized in the development of the largest branch of federal law enforcement to date: the Immigration and Customs Enforcement agency (ICE). This agency was developed in 2003 as the criminal justice arm of the Department of Homeland Security. "The reformation of the Immigration and Naturalization Service under the Department of Homeland Security (DHS) in 2003 was intended to consolidate a distinct regime of governance and statecraft at the hemispheric level, linked to the integration of markets, neoliberal restructuring, and military security across the region" (Camacho 7). According to Alicia Schmidt Camacho, the development of ICE was not merely about the development of protection. Rather, it was about the instantiation of neoliberal logics into the most basic of carceral governmental agencies. No longer is immigration policed by a separate entity; instead, it is joined together with fraud, gang taskforces, and sexual predators. The unifying identity of these varied perpatrators, however, is "foreign nationals."

The move to centralize all of these criminals under one large governmental agency may seem the antithesis of neoliberal privatization as described in chapter one. However, while its charge may group large swaths of crime under one umbrella, its reach is limited by key pieces of legislation that do not allow federal forces to enter state borders. In other words, as organized and clearly defined as ICE projects itself, it can do nothing without the assistance of intrastate and international cooperation. Therefore, it becomes critical that the message it circulates is one of personal responsibility and vigilance (much like the rhetoric provided by Bush post–9/11).

It appears in all of ICE's literature. As we analyze the information given by ICE itself, as well as the media coverage surrounding its various campaigns, we soon see that ICE, too, is an assemblage—one in which crime in the United States is both internal and external, foreign and domestic, and ultimately not tied to citizenship or non-citizenship at all. In fact, for ICE, much like the rhetoric in the Patriot Act, crime and criminality are not about identifying categorical group identities. Rather, they are about understanding how bodies become assembled brands, and then how those brands are used to police the United States as a whole.

That is exactly how ICE presents itself to the public—as an enforcement agency whose sole responsibility is keeping the United States safe by creating various task forces and operations that are aimed squarely at intercepting and gaining knowledge to intercept those who threaten the nation. ICE itself both maintains a website and produces many press releases to keep the public and the media apprised of the work they are doing to keep our citizenry safe. Their rhetoric, and subsequently the rhetoric of the media that covers the agency's raids and activities, first and foremost discusses the amount and types of arrests that they have made in their various operations.

For example, in an Associated Press article entitled "Hundreds of Illegal Immigrants are Seized in Sweep," which was reprinted throughout the United States, it becomes apparent that even though ICE's role as protector of the United States may be couched in terms of immigration, ICE is actually far more active in national criminal activities than the INS before them. The AP article states:

> In a blitz that began May 26, U.S. Immigration and Customs Enforcement has arrested nearly 2,100 illegal immigrants across the country. Officials said the raids are aimed at child molesters, gang members and other violent criminals, as well as people . . . who sneaked back into the country after a judge threw them out. ("Hundreds" A4)

The blitz described in this quote is presented as if it is a singular event or operation that began in May; however, when listing who is targeted, it becomes obvious that there are multiple targets that should be policed with vastly different protocols. The types of arrests, sentences, and tactics that are aimed at child molesters are very different than the ones aimed at immigrants who have been deported and return to the United States. What this description of the ICE raids does is equate the child molester, the gang member, and other violent criminals with illegal immigrants. This is a way to create association between different brands and connect them all with the "illegal immigrant." Through the rhetoric as well as the legal authority given to ICE as a government agency, immigration enforcement is becoming synonymous with violent and sexual crimes across the country.

Furthermore, part of the promise of arresting "illegal immigrants" is that not only will they be removed from society by being arrested, but they will be expelled from the nation through deportation. So ICE functions not only to help us define (as best we can) all the possible threats to our citizenry, but it also gives the promise of a nation free of threat because those threats will be removed. A *New York Times* article discusses the promise of deportation to "clean up" American streets. The article includes a quote from a high-ranking ICE official that explains how the

promise of deportation allows for a way to circumvent legal requirements and eliminate threats without the time or expense of a trial. "'A
person who's here illegally cannot hide behind the fact that he didn't
commit a felony,' Mr. Levy said. 'If you happen to be caught up, you
can't say that just because you haven't murdered someone you can get
around federal immigration laws'" (Healy L1.1).

Connecting immigration status to criminality is not a new phenomenon. In fact, ICE is merely drawing on the rhetoric of past attempts at
immigration reform. ICE's methods, however, are different than what we
have seen in the past. Instead of attempting to create sweeping legal
reform, ICE is attempting to use their newfound legal power to enforce
laws that already call for deportation of illegal immigration. Instead of
creating laws to change how immigrants are regulated, ICE is using law
enforcement as a means to regulate immigration. ICE bureaucratizes immigration reform by relocating the regulating of immigration from the
nation-state to municipalities and state agencies. Instead of being the
work of democratic lawmaking, immigration regulation is currently regulated by those who enact law instead of conceptualize it.

The bureaucratizing of immigration is not unprecedented. It draws on
the work of several states (not nation-states) that have proposed municipal legislation calling for criminalization of immigrants based on their
documentation status. Instead of waiting for federal reform, of which
immigration law has traditionally been the province, several states, such
as those discussed in chapter one, have attempted to create their own
initiatives to regulate the flow of immigrants past their borders. For example, as early as 1994, the Save our State (SOS) Initiative in California
attempted to pass Proposition 187 as a ballot measure. The rhetoric of the
proposition clearly defined undocumented immigrants as thieves who
threatened U.S. citizens' livelihoods and their way of life. This direct
connection between immigration and criminality created a connection
that is still seen, although not as directly, in the rhetoric of ICE today.
Proposition 187 states:

> SECTION 1. Findings and Declaration.
> The People of California find and declare as follows:
>
>> That they have suffered and are suffering economic hardship
>> caused by the presence of illegal aliens in this state.
>> That they have suffered and are suffering personal injury and dam-
>> age caused by the criminal conduct of illegal aliens in this state.
>> That they have a right to the protection of their government from
>> any person or persons entering this country unlawfully.
>
> Therefore, the People of California declare their intention to provide for
> cooperation between their agencies of state and local government with
> the federal government, and to establish a system of required notifica-
> tion by and between such agencies to prevent illegal aliens in the Unit-

ed States from receiving benefits or public services in the State of California. (Proposition 187)

The majority of people in favor of Proposition 187 were in favor of it on the grounds that illegal immigrants were breaking the law, and therefore, they should not be rewarded by the state for their non-disciplined behavior. After all, we needed to "Save our State" from the impending threat waiting at the border to come in and disrupt our way of life. The immigrant was framed as no more than a burglar waiting to enter the state. In other words, it was the responsibility of the state to discipline these law-breakers so that the general morality of the state would not be imperiled.

However, there is a greater significance to the language of the proposition. Not only did it serve to lay out seemingly rational arguments, but it framed those arguments as an affront to the nation, as if the nation was a home space which could be broken into or violated. The immigrants described in Proposition 187 were not merely immigrants who were entering the country unlawfully; they were bandits coming to steal our jobs and our culture, which as I noted earlier is a word that often serves to bring up images of women and children. Now immigrants are a direct threat to the national family because they are coming here to steal our livelihood and our culture.

Although ICE does not make such direct corollaries in defining immigrants as thieves, the fact that they are able to use their legal power to deport immigrants based solely on their immigration status (with no due process) shows that the connection between immigration and criminality is still viable. "The criminalized Latino/migrant thus constitutes the outside of the exclusionary juridical order, as the minimal subject whose expulsion and subjection to punishment calls it into being"(Camacho 15). Through its policing of undocumented workers, mothers, and migrants, ICE creates not only a link between criminality and immigrants, but it makes immigrants criminals purely through their institutional status. According to individual state regulations and ICE enforcement policy, immigrants must be deported because of their undocumented status only, not because of any crimes against private or public property.

So not only does ICE exploit the connections between violent, sexual crimes and immigration, but it also sets up a means to change the way these crimes are prosecuted. As long as there is suspicion that the perpetrator is illegal (and that can mean something as simple as expired papers), they can be removed from the United States. This changes the structures of legal rights and protection for criminals in this country, and more often than not (both in the media and now when brought before law enforcement) people are guilty without the luxury of getting to prove themselves innocent. These shifts establish a dangerous precedent in which law enforcement supersedes the juridical, and arrests and sentences become little more than bureaucratic paperwork.

ICE causes shifts in authority that impact U.S. citizens as well. In fact, ICE states that it is their job to protect U.S. citizens and in doing so, their jurisdiction often overlaps with issues of immigration. After all, ICE is the largest wing of the Department of Homeland Security, and protecting the homeland involves many levels of protection—family, community, and nation. Statements made by the director of Homeland Security Michael Chertoff, which were published in an ICE press release regarding identity theft, articulate the conflation of illegal immigration with privacy. He states: "Violations of our immigration laws and privacy rights often go hand in hand. . . . Enforcement actions like this one protect the privacy rights of innocent Americans while striking a blow against illegal immigration" ("Identity Theft"). In these two sentences, Chertoff establishes a link between the violation of privacy rights and immigration. Although the links may seem as if they are fallacious or contiguous reasoning, they are drawing on a deep history in which illegal immigrants have come to be known as personal threats to the private property of U.S. citizens.

By invoking these histories, Chertoff is relying on palimpsestic markings to help shore up his contiguous connection between immigration and property law. His comments work to join together undocumented immigrants and identity theft without articulating the complicating factor that immigrants are only using social security numbers to gain employment. There has been much research done by independent presses and immigrant rights groups, which has shown that the majority of "stolen social security numbers" are not used in order to build credit debt, but rather to gain employment due to new ICE regulations for employers. The identity theft which was the basis of many meatpacking plant raids in 2007 has been connected to the use of social security numbers in employment data bases, not fraudulent credit card use. However, the main usage in the media of the term "identity theft" denotes the stealing of personal credit cards to make large purchases. These are not the same practices, although Chertoff seeks to occlude those differences. This is the way the rhetoric of assemblage works, much like the newly formed ICE agency itself. By putting crimes, and thus criminals, under the same umbrella it creates associations between these crimes that are rhetorically, but not materially, there.

Assembling immigrants, computer hackers, and those who commit fraud together under one large security apparatus creates the potential for slippage between each group. Instead of the brand of immigrant maintaining its clear definitional content, it begins to be associated with the criminal behaviors of the others policed by ICE. Therefore, it becomes easy to view immigration status in itself as criminal because it is policed by the same enforcement agency that protects us from "identity theft" and "large scale computer hacking." Both of those crimes carry a level of malfeasance that lack of documentation does not. But assembling undocumented immigrants with the brands of "computer hacker" and "identity thief" allows for contiguous associations to be made, thus affecting how we *feel* about immigrants. They become equally as suspicious as those stealing our credit cards or hacking into the Pentagon. At the very least, they become equally threatening to the U.S. nation-state.

ASSEMBLING THE NATION: COMPLICATING THE CITIZEN/NON-CITIZEN DIVIDE

ICE attempts not only to create a new interlocking set of threats. It also attempts to create its own interlocking model of law enforcement. After all, if the threats are becoming more comprehensive, our criminal justice system must not allow issues such as national boundaries or the nature of jurisdiction to stop the apprehension and expulsion of threats. This new model allows for connections between municipal, state, and federal law enforcement, as well as international taskforces that establish links between foreign law enforcement bodies. For example, the information statement on ICE's Operation Predator discusses the ways in which ICE's connections to foreign law enforcement agencies, as well as foreign governments, enable them to better apprehend criminals at home and abroad. The website states:

> Working cooperatively with foreign governments through ICE attaché offices worldwide, ICE agents have made more than 196 arrests under the child sex tourism provisions of the PROTECT Act. For example, on May 19, 2006, SAC/Los Angeles agents brought evidence before a federal grand jury in the Central District of California that resulted in the indictment of Steven Eric Prowler. Prowler was indicted on charges that he engaged in illicit sex acts in a foreign place. Prowler was deported from Thailand after serving one year in a Thai prison for sexual encounters with approximately 100 underage Thai boys.[3] ("Predator")

In addition to expelling those ("illegal immigrants") who are seen as threats, ICE polices people who very much belong (citizens) even when they are outside of our national boundaries. This shift seems as if it makes sense because it is policing U.S. citizens for behaviors that would not be accepted at home. So why should they be accepted abroad? However, it creates a legal precedent that allows the United States to enter into other countries and exercise the rule of law within that nation's boundaries in the name of U.S. law and morality. In other words, through the work of ICE, the United States is allowed to police its own borders by expelling those who are "illegal" or perform "illegal" acts, *and* they are allowed to police their own citizens and legal immigrants outside of the United States, thus becoming a supra-national legal entity.

Prowler's case reaffirms that sexual practice, as discussed in chapter two, is a key means in regulating the borders of the nation-state. Historically, it has been used as a way to regulate who comes into the country.

For example, The National Public Health Services 1987 prohibition was turned into law in 1993, and it prevented immigrants with HIV from entering the country and/or applying for citizenship. It states:

> Sec. 2007 Exclusion of Aliens Infected with the Agent for Acquired Immune Deficiency Syndrome
>
> a. Exclusion of Aliens on Health-Related Grounds—Section 212 (a)(1)(A)(i) of the Immigration and Nationality Act (8 U.S.C. 1182) (a)(1)(A)(i) is amended by adding at the end of the following: 'which shall include infection with the etiologic agent for acquired immune deficiency syndrome.'
> b. Effective Dated—The amendment made by subsection (a) shall take effect 30 days after the date of the enactment of this Act.

The language of the law was banal enough, but the ban was not against all kinds of illness. It was specifically against those with AIDS. There were no stipulations as to when or if tests would be administered to determine if an immigrant had the disease. However, there were already procedures in place where immigrants applying for legal status had to submit to blood testing. As Jonathan Rauch, senior writer for the *National Journal* who is quoted on the *Act Up* website, states:

> The policy never required an HIV test for entry; only when an alien seeks permanent-resident status, usually after having already been in the country for years, is the blood test routinely required. So the policy, as put into practice, is about kicking people out, not keeping them in. ("HIV Immigration and Travel")

In effect, the prohibition turned law was a means of targeting specific bodies from particular groups and specific locations that had historically been tied to the AIDS epidemic. But even more sinister, it was a means of removing those bodies already within our immigration system that the country wanted out. Most often those bodies represented raced foreign nationals who had already been constructed throughout the history of AIDS as dangerous.[4]

There was a strong push in the early 1990s, and it looked as if President Clinton was going to overturn the National Health Service's prohibition. That was until 1991, following after the bloody overthrow of Jean-Bertrand Aristide, when thousands of Haitians flocked to the United States seeking asylum. Unfortunately Haiti and those who occupied that territory had a particular place in the U.S. imaginary when it came to AIDS, and 268 male refugees were detained without charges at Guantanamo Bay, Cuba on the suspicion that they were infected with HIV. Many of those detained faced

> [O]penly discriminatory . . . policies, [when] the INS also sanctioned the isolation of HIV-positive Haitian refugees in special cells at Guantanamo. . . . [T]hroughout the 1980s, and even into the 1990s, Haitians

had openly been targeted by the Centers for Disease Control as one of
the 4H's (homosexuals, hemophiliacs, heroin users, and Haitians),
those negatively labeled as HIV carriers. (Braziel 136)

It is interesting to note, however, that Haitians were the only ethnic
group who by nature of their race, not behavior or needs, were labeled
high risk. Many other "African" or "African identified" ethnicities were
hailed as "carriers" or "vectors" of the disease. Several reasons were put
forth to justify these assumptions—poverty, lack of medical care, and
African sexual practices (Patton, *Inventing Aids*). Additionally, because
AIDS allegedly originated in Africa, there was the belief that those of
African descent possessed a certain genetic mutation or immunological
change that sparked the transmission of the disease. In other words,
Africans carried on their bodies the orginary myth of AIDS, making them
the ultimate brands (Watney, "The Spectacle of AIDS").

Simon Watney reminds us of both the colonial and racist roots of
African AIDS. He states: "Secular institutions appropriate and refashion
an equally sober discourse of 'promiscuity,' which drifts out across the
Mediterranean to incorporate the entire African subcontinent and beyond, recharging 'the orient' with a deadly cargo of exoticism that reminds 'us' that negritude has always been, for whites, a sign of sexual
excess and death" (74). For Watney, the connection made between
African bodies and the circulation of AIDS speaks to the deeply held
racist histories and beliefs still circulating throughout the West. It is the
faulty construction between race and behavior that is critical here because it was not only Africans who were named as possibly dangerous
foreign nationals.

There was also a great deal of misinformation surrounding sex workers, especially in Asia. These women were seen as receptacles for the
disease because although they could not transmit it through vaginal
intercourse (or so it was believed then) they practiced anal sex, so they
were not only at risk of catching the disease, but also passing it on. In
1985, Walter Reed Hospital in Maryland conducted a study involving
self-identified heterosexual U.S. military men who tested positive for
HIV antibodies, and the men reported that they had in fact practiced anal
sex with sex workers in Asia. Cindy Patton describes the study and asks
some very provocative questions that reveal how foreign bodies are used
to mask our own socially stigmatized sexual behavior. She states, "Wom-
en, especially sex workers, immediately came to be viewed as the 'vector'
moving HIV from the sex and drug underworld to the heterosexual men,
who then passed it on to their wives, the 'vessels' of procreation" (39).
Even abroad, foreign-born women could threaten the women of our
country and therefore the procreative possibilities of American citizens. It
is easy, then, to see that if risky behavior is exoticized and racialized, we
must close the gates in order to protect national family and its women

and unborn children when confronted with these bodies attempting to enter our country.

Former Californian Representative Robert Dornan articulated these very anxieties in an impassioned plea to reject the amnesty request of several Haitian men who requested entrance into the United States. He stated, "What we're talking about is letting people come into this country in their young years—what liberals call raging hormones, sexually active years (look at the profile of Haitians) with a communicable, venereal disease that is always fatal. I'm not just isolating this disease or isolating Haitians; if they were all little redheads [we would still keep them out]" (ACT UP New York website). Yet there have been thousands of "little redheads" who have entered the country without suspicion or request to submit to a blood test. This is where the inaccuracy of the language of the law reveals just what Rep. Dorman is attempting to dispel; there are certain bodies who must be kept out because of who they are, not what they do. These bodies, as Watney makes clear, are often Africans or Asians because those are the exotic bodies who are marked to behave culturally suspect.

But it is not only exotic bodies who become coded as culturally suspect. The exotic locales from which those bodies hail are also seen as site of questionable conduct.[5] As such, U.S. citizens who travel to these countries must be protected when abroad as well. Therefore, ICE developed new policing mechanisms to not only expel threats from and/or protect the U.S. border from threatening immigrants, but also to patrol U.S. citizens *and* legal immigrants as they leave the United States for countries abroad. In other words, ICE is relying on the historical notion of protecting the United States from sexual practices deemed deviant and using that precedent to extend the range of U.S. authority outside of U.S. borders. All of this is clearly seen within the rhetoric of the Protect Act. This law demonstrates how palimpsestic meaning is rhetorically mobilized through branding in order to gain material control across the globe. The purpose of the Protect Act was to insure that children at home or abroad are protected from sexual abuse. The act covers not only child sexual abuse at home, but also those who travel and commit sexual acts with minors while abroad. The act states:

> Travel with intent to engage in illicit sexual conduct.—A person who travels in interstate commerce or travels into the United States, or a United States Citizen or an alien admitted for permanent residence in the United States who travels in foreign commerce, for the purpose of engaging in any illicit sexual conduct with another person shall be fined under this title or imprisoned not more than 30 years, or both. (Sec. 105, b)

Even if the U.S. citizen or permanent legal resident did not travel with the primary intent to engage in illicit conduct, but does end up doing so while in a foreign nation, the act accounts for that happening, as well. It states:

> Engaging in illicit sexual conduct in foreign places.—Any United States citizen or alien admitted for permanent residence who travels in foreign commerce, and engages in any illicit sexual conduct with another person shall be fined under this title or impressing not more than 30 years, or both. (Sec 105, c)

Together these two sections outline both the infraction of illicit sexual behavior and the consequence. It also combines two classes of U.S. residents that have radically different legal rights and recognition. Citizens are different than those who possess Green Cards for the basic reason that those with Green Cards can have them revoked, and citizens are citizens until they disavow or petition to become a citizen of another nation. In other words, ICE can now police U.S. citizens who would go to jail *and* permanent legal residents who could be deported if they are arrested in the United States and beyond. The development of ICE, then, collapses several juridical classifications: 1) it collapses types of criminality and crimes, 2) it collapses discrete sites of jurisdiction, and 3) it collapses the categories of citizenship and immigration. All of these collapses create situations in which figures and identifiers become cloudy and hard to keep apart from one another.

The passage of the Protect Act and the formation of ICE demonstrate how the assembling of brands is changing how the U.S. nation-state is defining legal citizen and immigrant categories as well. In fact, the Protect Act spends a great deal of time designating just what is considered illicit sexual behavior, and never works to define just what is the difference between a citizen, permanent legal resident, or illegal immigrant. This shift in over-determining the action and not the identity of those who commit the action is another feature of the rhetoric of terror. The law states:

> Definition,—As used in this section, the term 'illicit sexual conduct' means (1) a sexual act (as defined in section 2246) with a person under 18 years of age that would be in violation of chapter 109A if the sexual act occurred in the special maritime and territorial jurisdiction of the United States; or (2) any commercial sex act (as defined in section 1591) with a person under 18 years of age. (Sec 105, f)

The law is defining "illicit sexual acts" in the context of the laws in the United States. This means that even if a country, such as Thailand, has laws that allow for sexual contact, commercial or otherwise, between minors and adults, someone traveling from the United States would need to abide by the United States's legal definition of "illicit sexual acts." The U.S. traveler carries the laws of the United States on their body, across national borders, allowing for the United States to spread its morality and legalities across the world on the bodies of its citizens. Therefore, the responsibility of being a U.S. citizen, or even permanent legal resident, becomes much more about carrying the nation-state with you, instead of the nation protecting you wherever you go.

It is also of note that the definition of "illicit sexual acts" is tied to both age and the commodification of sex. In this sense the definition of citizenship remains by nature one of consumerism, but it also becomes about the commodification and export of U.S. morality. In other words, if a citizen recognizes the severe punishment that they could face for participating in "illicit sex," they may not travel and/or attempt to purchase sex. If the United States can encourage its citizens to abstain from purchasing sex abroad, the sex tourism industry could be slowed by an economic downturn. This reading, however, presupposes that the main reason to prosecute sexual predators abroad is about national image and relations, but in fact, it is more about asserting a model of behavior for U.S. citizens and legal residents that eschews ill morals and behaves appropriately. "We want this to serve as a deterrent, we want to get the message out that any American that molests children anywhere in the world, we will actively pursue them, investigate the case and prosecute them in the United States," says Ann Hurst, a Bangkok-based official with ICE ("LA Man Faces Charges" 1).

The policing of what is appropriate and what is not can be seen in ICE's policies of both sex travel abroad and the trafficking of sexual images at home. In fact, one of ICE's main objectives in "Operation Predator" is to end the circulation of child pornography over the Internet. Here is another example of the shifting boundaries of ICE. ICE proclaims, and its name supports, that it is interested in pursuing and eliminating foreign nationals who commit violent and/or sexual crimes in the United States. Its claim is that "U.S. customs officials, who have taken an increasing role in Internet-based child pornography because it crosses international borders" (Thermos B4). It is this connection to the international through the circulation of information—not bodies—across the Internet that ICE can maintain its jurisdiction in U.S.-based child pornography cases. After all, the images and server hosting is often offshore, so the crime is international, even if the perpetrator is not. So ICE becomes the default agency to police sexual misconduct both at home and abroad.

As ICE begins to change how U.S. citizens' sexual conduct is policed across the globe, it also is changing how the legal process is enacted for immigrants within the United States. Because of the bureaucratization of immigration, most foreign nationals do not receive a trial and are deported based on suspicion only. In a press release about a sexual predator arrested in Salinas, CA, ICE officials outline the importance of fighting predatory behavior. It states:

> "Pedophiles pose a serious threat to the well-being of our children, our families, and our communities," said Charles DeMore, special agent-in-

charge for the ICE office of investigations in San Francisco, which oversees the agency's Salinas office as well. "We will continue to work
closely with our law enforcement partners to target those who prey on
the children of this community. In the case of foreign nationals who
commit predatory offenses, we can not only take them off the streets,
but we can seek to have them sent out of the country." ("40 Salinas
Residents")

The reference to foreign nationals is interesting because it implies that
foreign national sexual predators are the exception for which they have a
strategy, not the normative pattern of arrest. By including immigration,
illicit sexual acts, and child pornography under one law enforcement
agency, the lines between citizen and non-citizen are further compromised, and often the only way to tell the difference is whether they are
arrested or deported.

The development of ICE as an über-transnational law enforcement
agency is borne out of the need to police the terrorist who is a criminal
who is often unrecognizable among us. So not only are there terrorists
among us who we cannot identify, there are also predators who are prey-
ing on our children. The predator is in our neighborhoods,[6] and invading
our homes through the Internet. Wendy Koch discusses the difficulty in
profiling the sexual predator, and affirms that a predator could be anyone, anywhere. She states:

> "The frightening thing about this is the only commonality they share is
> this interest in child sex abuse," says Jane Wilcox, chief of the Toronto
> police sex crimes unit that began the investigation. "They run the gam-
> ut. You can't develop a profile of this type of person, because it could
> be anybody," she says. (Koch A3)

The unidentifiable nature of the predator is what makes it so dangerous,
and what makes ICE, who have been trained by Homeland Security to
secure our borders from terrorism, a natural fit to investigate and prosecute these cases. In other words, ICE has become the default agency not
only to produce the rhetoric to teach people how to police themselves
against amorphous threats, but also protect our nation by enforcing appropriate behavior at home and abroad. They do this by assembling
brands. It is not enough that ICE has become the über-agency for surveillance, but they also must justify their amalgamation of responsibilities by
demonstrating how each brand is *equally* as dangerous as any other. The
contiguous connections between brands allow for the slippage of meaning that creates assembled brands and these assembled threats pose even
greater threats than the brands do on their own.

It makes perfect sense, then, that *this* agency is in charge of sex crimes,
violent crimes, gang crime, and immigration violations. All of these "categories" of crime have one major thing in common. They describe behaviors that cannot be easily attached to particular bodies or groups. The

predator, gang-banger, illegal alien, and terrorist are all new brands borne of uncertainty and anxiety in our post–9/11 world. When assembled, they create not only new forms of threat that are ever-present and pervasive, but they also create the need for an agency that can help protect us and help us protect ourselves from these dangerous figures.

All of the criminals who are prosecuted under the jurisdiction of ICE are presented as threats to safety, and often those threats are explained in terms of economics and property. Whether the threats are being discussed in the context of "Operation Predator," "Immigration Enforcement," or "Operation Community Shield," which monitors gang activity that has transnational ties across the globe, these threats are presented as threats to our property and thus threats to public safety. In the context of gang crime, the biggest threat posed by gangs is not deaths caused by gang warfare, but it is actually the property loss and damage committed by gangs. "'The gangs commit acts of violence wherever they are. They rob. They do carjacking. They do drive-by shootings,' Arnold said. 'They're a threat to public safety'" (Finley C02). Although drive-by shootings are violent crimes, the other threats to public safety listed here are crimes of property. This focus on property connects citizenship back to consumerism, and thus creates a way to commodify public safety.

ASSEMBLING CONSUMERS: SELLING ICE AS *THE* BRAND OF PROTECTION

But perhaps the most chilling connection between safety and property is the discussion of how ICE works to keep our streets safe for our children. In a press release about a major child pornography bust in Houston, Texas, the special agent in charge of the case clearly connects children and property.

> "We must protect our most valuable assets, our children, from predators who sexually exploit them," said Bob Rutt, special agent in charge of the ICE Office of Investigations in Houston. "The ICE investigation which led to this lengthy prison sentence illustrates our commitment to removing sexual predators from our streets to make our communities safer for everyone, especially children." ("Houston" 1)

Children are no longer mere victims in need of our saving or protection; they are now our most valuable property. By describing the protection of children in terms of economics and property, Rutt's comments reveal the deeply economic nature of all of these brands of terror and protection. We are told to be afraid of particular behaviors because they can harm us, but the harm that is most dangerous to the United States is the damage to our belief in private property and accumulation. If our children, our identities, our communities are described as our greatest assets it is because without them the U.S. economic system cannot continue.

We are a nation of consumers, and even though the branding of terror attempts to shift those responsibilities to a nation of policing bodies, we are still assured that if we protect what is ours—our home, our family, and our children—we will be free. It is ICE's job to both create and destroy our invisible threats, in order to define how they are both at once eminent and ephemeral. It is the unsettling nature of the unknown that we must overcome and for which we must overcompensate. Therefore, we forfeit our rights, we police our own neighborhoods, and we vote more conservatively in order to maintain the lifestyle to which we have grown accustomed. The branding of terror and protection helps make our choices more invisible by clouding the economic and political identities of so-called dangerous bodies.

NOTES

1. What becomes interesting is the way in which contiguous reasoning, which I am examining as particular to the assemblage in this chapter, functions not only in association with identities and individual threat. Think of the Bush administration's reasoning for invading Iraq. It was not based on logic or the demonstration of fact, but rather it was the repetition of the meme that Saddam Hussein was involved with al-Qaeda. Even now, when this has been proven inaccurate, there are some who still hold on to this tenuous connection to justify our presence in Iraq.

2. One thing that is important to note in Puar and Rai's description of the new processes of patriotism is the fact that even though the brand of the terrorist has begun to unmoor the dangerous traits from particular raced, gendered, or sexualized bodies, it also reifies those connections by drawing on the colonial histories and relationships that have structured the nature of those stereotypes for many years. But it is not only how the brand of the terrorist-monster recalls older histories, what is important is that these brands draw together those historically stereotypical traits to create new brands of threats that contain racial, gendered, and sexualized characteristics, which are assembled together as disembodied, combined, and rebodied brands.

3. It is important to note that Prowler was arrested in Thailand for illicit sexual conduct, specifically for having sex with teenage boys. This is a site where the heteropatriarchy of the state becomes apparent. Thailand is a site where there is a booming sex tourism industry that exploits teenage girls. It is a large part of the nation's economic growth and progress. The fact that Prowler was arrested and then extradited to the United States had everything do with the fact that he was having relations with boys and not girls. In other words, if he had been having sex with girls, underage or not, he would have never been arrested. Economics is tied to gender and heterosexuality in the neoliberal economy.

4. See *Inventing AIDS* by Cindy Patton.

5. Both M. Jaqui Alexander and Jasbir Puar along with several other transnational queer theorists have written extensively about "sex tourism." For Puar, these are vacation packages which sell romance and/or the freedom of the exotic to Western travelers. For Alexander it is the politics and histories of the Caribbean that lead to national economies based in travel and entertainment. Both examples create uneven relationships between the West and "exotic lands" that are sutured to pleasure and entertainment.

6. Megan's Law, passed in 1994, created a database which is accessible to anyone with a computer in the United States. This database lists the names and addresses of those convicted of sex crimes. This enables parents to see when a sexual predator is living within their neighborhood. This knowledge presumably helps them keep their

children safer. What becomes even more interesting is that this type of surveillance allows for the new watchful policing citizen that supports and was created by the branding of terror.

FOUR

"José Padilla" and "Osama bin Laden"

Material Consequences of Branding Bodies

TERRORISM, JOSÉ PADILLA, AND OSAMA BIN LADEN: OR HOW WE LOST OUR HUMANITY

In chapter one, I discussed how the shift from a disciplinary society to a society of control enables branding and rhetorical assemblage to evacuate both objects and bodies of their material value. Although chapter two explained how the branding of terror reestablishes a national identity by invoking "family" and "protection" and chapter three demonstrated how the branded threats are assembled to further the rhetoric of national security, neither chapter fully engaged with the material consequences for those bodies who are used and assembled as brands. This chapter will focus on the material costs of branding by analyzing the rhetoric of two very material situations—the incarceration of José Padilla and the killing of Osama bin Laden.

Both of these events are tied to the September 11th attacks, and both events are rhetorically branded within the context of terror and protection. However, what the branding of the terms "José Padilla" and "Osama bin Laden" occludes is the humanity of the men who reside in the actual bodies—not the branded ones. And as such, the rhetoric surrounding both Padilla's incarceration and bin Laden's killing mystifies the actual material circumstances and conditions of each event, leaving empty shells with only representational value.

Yet each event is a material event. Incarceration, torture without access to due process, death—these are distinctly human experiences. They affect lives and bodies quite intimately. And no matter how branded each man becomes—whether in name or political label—the stories of those experiences begin to disrupt the seamless devaluation of their humanity that is central to the process of branding. Instead, the material conditions of these brands lead to a series of confused and contradictory news items reported in each case. In both instances, the more information given on each story, the more confused the stories become. It is my contention that it is not because of purposeful occlusion or misreporting, but rather it is the juxtaposition of the material circumstances with the brand that creates such strong conflict within each story, so much so it becomes hard to parse the facts or create coherence.

The chapter, then, looks at the arrest and incarceration (and subsequent torture) of José Padilla within the borders of the United States and the assassination of Osama bin Laden in northern Pakistan. Both of these bodies are used by the nation-state to solidify its power and identity after the 9/11 attacks. In Padilla's case, he was considered an "enemy combatant" at first, but soon, he was assembled into a brand unto himself. In the case of bin Laden, he was branded from the beginning not only as a terrorist, as discussed in chapter three, but as the über-terrorist who threatened all Western ideologies. Both of these men, I argue, because of their branded identities, are subject to very material consequences.

The idea is that a "terrorist" (suspected or otherwise) is not worthy of humane treatment because terror demonstrates the ultimate lack of humanity. And the ultimate terrorist, as this chapter will discuss, is Osama bin Laden. In the ten years since the September 11th attacks, bin Laden has become less of a man, and more of a brand unto himself. He is the face of terrorism, and the face upon which we must seek revenge for the crimes committed against the United States as a whole. Even as intelligence came through that bin Laden the man was no longer primarily in control of the day-to-day operations of al-Qaeda, he still functioned in the imaginary of the U.S. public as a bogeyman of sorts. His assassination, then, functioned less as a blow to terrorism, and more as a symbolic ending to a decade of fear and revenge fantasies.

And although not all terrorists are über-terrorists, as I will argue, the fear of terrorism produces material effects for all global citizens. In fact, the term "enemy combatant" was created and made a legal category, through the Patriot Act of 2001, as a means of stripping suspected terrorists of all national citizenship and any rights therein. However that term, as we have seen with the horrors attached to Abu Ghraib and the stateside torture of José Padilla, also strips those so designated of the basic human rights, histories, and compassions that are expected to be given to our fellow man regardless of their citizenship status.

The addition of the category "enemy combatant" to the policing of terrorism further erodes the nation-state's basic agreements with its constituents. No longer can individual citizens rely on the liberally defined social contract he/she has with the state. The social contract assumes that the state will insure access to basic civil rights and needs for all of its citizens. With the policing of enemy combatants and terrorists, not to mention the erosion of basic services and availability of jobs articulated in chapter one, U.S. citizens cannot assume that the state will insure basic civil or human rights. They can, however, feel secure in the fact that the state is policing them and their neighbors. And it is that contradiction of the loss of state supported civil rights and the increase of state police protection that intensifies the fear and anxieties around the branding of terror.

Yet, as discussed in chapter three, it is with the very promise of protection, through the expulsion of these brands, that the state reifies its national power in the eyes of its citizens. The enemy combatant, and I would argue the terrorist, become the branded exceptions post–9/11. As discussed in chapter one, exceptions to state law serve to define the state through their expulsion or ultimate assimilation. In the case of enemy combatants, however, it is not enough to remove these bodies from the country or assimilate them through incarceration. Instead, these exceptions must be eradicated or erased to demonstrate the state's ability to protect itself and its subjects from threat. The brands "enemy combatant" and "terrorist," then, remove all humanity and civil rights, even from those whom the state is constructed to protect, with no option of recovery or rehabilitation. Instead, these bodies must be *disappeared*.[1] Giorgio Agamben calls these beings "bare life."

For Agamben, bare life is a being who must be killed so that the state may remain whole. Bare life is *homo sacer*—a human who may be killed but not sacrificed. This difference may seem insignificant; however, according to Agamben, it means that the death of the victim will not reestablish or regenerate society. Instead, the victim lives a life of exile, one in which he cannot be killed with impunity, like a sacrifice, but must be killed in order to keep the appearance of the civil order. He states:

> What is captured in the sovereign ban is a human victim who may be killed but not sacrificed: *homo sacer*. . . . The life caught in the sovereign ban is the life that is originarily sacred—that is, that may be killed but not sacrificed—and, in this sense, the production of bare life is the originary activity of sovereignty. (83)

Homo Sacer, according to Agamben, comes from an obscure Roman rite that defines said person as "able to be killed but not sacrificed," and therefore not able to participate in any religious rites or possess any civil liberties (82). The human victim is banned from participation in the sovereign state, but still must be punished under sovereign law. According to Agamben, this is the original contradiction in democracy, and it demonstrates how deeply intertwined democracy, sovereignty, and human life really are.

Additionally, Agamben uses the presence of bare life to illustrate how it is an "exception" that is more than an exception, but instead a limit of sovereignty within democratic societies. The contradiction present in the life that cannot be valued but that must be ended provides a clear example of how sovereign states can no longer rely on exile to reify their borders. Instead they rely on the exertion of "force of law" in order to demonstrate their totalizing power both within and beyond the state's borders. I discussed this phenomenon in chapter three in my discussion of the development of ICE and its ability to police U.S. citizens across the globe. And although that discussion did not focus on criminals who would be put to death, it did present a contradiction of sovereignty wherein the United States extended its power through the bodies of its citizens, all the while revoking the civil rights of those citizens.

The presence of bare life within discussions of sovereignty would seem to be a contradiction within the context of the neoliberal nation-state, as I have articulated it in chapter one. If Deleuze's claim of a society of control is accurate, then why would a nation-state need to assert its own control through bare life, branding or other means? What branding (throughout the book) and bare life (in this particular chapter) demonstrate is that although we have moved toward a society of control, there are still many affective registers that seek the appearance of a strong centralized nation-state. Branding of bodies is a technology of neoliberal governmentality. It succeeds in an era of threat because it allows for a focus on the affective threats, and not the material realities of neoliberalism. It is through branding that the material manifestations, such as ICE discussed in chapter three, are still relevant.

Padilla and bin Laden, as "enemy combatant" and "terrorist" respectively, are both brands and examples of bare life. And through an analysis of their media representations, I will show the material effects that result from contradictions of the sovereign assertion of power in a time of neoliberal economics. These very contradictions are central to the flux of neoliberalism, and it is often through the means of branding that the state attempts to erase those contradictions and produce simple, *affective* rhetorics. But Agamben's bare life can illuminate the material and rhetorical conjunctures between representation and power present in neoliberalism.

PADILLA: (DIS)ASSEMBLING THE THREAT

José Padilla, a.k.a. Abdullah al-Muhajir or Muhajir Abdullah, has been at the center of one of the most controversial terrorism cases post–9/11. Even though by the time of his initial detainment in 2002 there had been several other highly publicized "enemy combatant" cases (for example, John Walker Lindh), Padilla became uniquely meaningful to both the conservative and liberal media, as well as to politicians. For the conservatives, he was our country's worst nightmare—a U.S. citizen born of immigrant parents, who turned to Islam, and subsequently to terrorism, while in prison attempting to atone for his gang-banger past. For the liberals, he was an example of the Bush administration's assault on the civil liberties of U.S. citizens with the adoption of the Patriot Act.

Padilla's case, and eventually Padilla himself, represented the struggle between the citizenry's desire for freedom versus its need to feel protected. At least that is how the media and the government portrayed the stakes of the case. Padilla was characterized as a homegrown terrorist who demonstrated that terror is no longer the sole province of foreign bodies or foreign nationals. Instead, terrorism could be cultivated within the borders of the United States and performed by U.S. citizens. Through the discussions of due process and civil rights, as well as the discussion of terrorist activity right here at home, the Padilla case began to reveal how the branding of protection and the branding of terror did not always work in concert with one another.

Common themes in the media discussion surrounding Padilla offer two distinct narratives about his worth to the war on terror and as a U.S. citizen.[2] In a *USA Today* article published on 12 July 2002, Johnson and Diamond reported on a press conference given by then Attorney General John Ashcroft. His comments and how they were reported are very much in line with the branding of terror which I have discussed in chapters two and three. Ashcroft's comments serve to raise the intensity of the threat of terror by claiming that al-Qaeda is not only the province of foreign terrorists, but ones that are U.S.-based as well. The article states:

> Attorney General John Ashcroft said Thursday that al-Qaeda maintains a "hidden but active presence" in the USA and that its members are poised to strike again. "As we limit the access of foreign terrorists to our country," Ashcroft said, "we recognize that the terrorists' response will be to recruit United States citizens and permanent residents to carry out their attacks." (Johnson and Diamond A-02)

Many conservative media outlets and web-based discussion groups used the idea of recruitment of U.S. citizens and permanent residents to undermine the rights of those citizens accused of terrorist activity. The accusation of terror spawned a discussion in which the perpetrator was guilty from the beginning, prompting speculation as to why a citizen would turn to terror, and what should happen to said citizen now that they had become an enemy of the state. The conversations surrounding the Padilla case within conservative presses and discussion groups followed these two trends fairly faithfully.

Early in Padilla's detainment, discussion in the liberal media concerned his rights as a citizen, and they saw his detainment without sentence and/or trial as a direct breach of the civil liberties which are supposed to be afforded to all U.S. citizens. It mattered not to the liberal press whether Padilla was guilty or innocent. It was his treatment at the hands of the government that was of primary concern. In an article published in *The Christian Science Monitor*, Warren Richey analyzed Padilla's case as a potential watershed moment in policing in the name of terror. His take was not positive, but it was a means of warning other liberals of the dangers surrounding the case of a U.S. citizen who was essentially disappeared by his government without due process.[3] Richey writes:

> In effect, the Padilla case may ultimately help make the world safer for use of coercive interrogation tactics. It could do so, analysts say, by establishing legal precedents that insulate military interrogations from scrutiny by civilian judges in federal courts. (Richey 01)

Richey is laying out the stakes associated with the Padilla case in no uncertain terms. He sees it as a moment that the government could use to reinforce its erosion of civil liberties quite decisively. Padilla may just be the first of many, and because the government and the media have constructed his case in terms of his deviance, many have been reluctant to question the government's non-standard procedures of detainment in this case. Richey's assertion about the dire civil consequences surrounding the Padilla case circulated throughout mainstream and independent media outlets, and there were many passionate discussions about how Padilla's plight represented a potential assault on all U.S. citizens, supported by an "unscrupulous administration" and the Patriot Act. For the liberal media, Padilla was a clear example of these breaches of the rights of citizens.

Both of these narratives about Padilla can be seen throughout the duration of his detainment and subsequent trial. Padilla became less of a subject in these articles and more of a brand, one that served to contextualize and launch discussions of the dangers of terror in the United States. One example of Padilla being used to brand terror can be seen in an early article in *USA Today*. The authors of the article discuss the ways in which Padilla's past made him a mark for al-Qaeda. They state: "José Padilla was just a troubled kid from the streets of Chicago. But his brushes with the law apparently made him a fertile target for recruitment by radical Muslims. What's more, his U.S. passport would have made him a valuable asset for al-Qaeda" (Wiseman et al. A03). The Wiseman article uses Padilla to forward an argument about how at-risk youth in the United States are a prime target for terrorist activity. In this construction of Padilla as "fertile ground" and a "valuable asset," all agency is removed from Padilla the man. Instead, Padilla becomes a cautionary tale of the risks and consequences of crime and disenfranchised youth.

In this report, Padilla is described as a gang-banger turned terrorist, possessing the qualities of gang-youth culture, previously alluded to in chapter three. Therefore, not only does this article rely on previous brands (the gang-banger) and the history of crime contained therein. It also assembles a new brand by connecting Padilla's gang past to his alleged terrorist present. These connections function to obviate any critical discussion of Padilla's crime or detainment. Padilla is not the true subject of this investigation, but instead, he functions as a means to discuss the state of terror in the United States.

Padilla's past gang activity served as an explanation for his terrorist behavior even in liberal publications. An in-depth article in *The Christian Science Monitor* attempts to portray Padilla in a sympathetic light, all the while explaining the ways in which the United States is vulnerable to terrorists within its borders due to the disenfranchisement of migrants, transients, and gang members. The authors report:

> It's on the ghetto street corner that many experts believe Al Qaeda could find its most fertile recruiting ground. Gang members and others who feel disenfranchised often lack some sort of support system, such as friends or family, and they may be thousands of miles away from home. "The disproportionate number of disaffected are transients, newcomers, migrants," says Jack Levin of the Brudnick Center on Violence at Northeastern University in Boston. "When things go bad, to them it seems catastrophic, and they become vulnerable," he says. (Scherer and Marks 2)

Through the inclusion of Levin's comments, Scherer and Marks have used expert testimony to support the assertion presented here and in the *USA Today* article (as well as many other articles reporting on Padilla's initial detention) that Padilla's past and socio-economic and citizenship status led him to join al-Qaeda. Again, there is no discussion about possible motives or rationale. Instead, Padilla is a man trapped by his upbringing and lifestyle. These brands evoke many we have seen earlier about lifestyle and behavior contaminating one's future, and thus contaminating the United States.

These assertions are different than those of the terrorist assemblage discussed in chapter three. They are attached to groups of identities but never to the larger systems of power or oppression. The "ghetto" isn't just a space in a city. Rather, it is a space produced by economic redlining, section 8 building approvals, and institutional racism. Levin not only avoids discussion of economic and institutional responsibility, but also lists "immigrants and newcomers" as threats equal to transients and gang members because of the lack of systematic support for all of these groups. So immigrants, much like gang members (both of whom were discussed in chapter three as groups policed by ICE), lack the necessary support and are therefore equally threatening to the U.S. population. Once again, we see the "other" named and blamed for the lack of homeland security in the United States, and Padilla, even though he is a citizen by birth, is implicated in these threats through his connection to terror both inside and outside the United States. We also clearly see the use of branded groupings in connection with his story present in the article.

The circulation of these narratives can be seen throughout the media, but they can also be seen in the commentary made by individuals about the case. A letter to the editor that ran in the *New York Times* on June 12, 2002, demonstrates how the narrative of Padilla's transformation from gang member to terrorist resonated with the U.S. public.[4] The letter presents a narrative in which Padilla's specific story is abstracted to a general principle in which all U.S. prisoners have the potential to become terrorists. The letter reads:

> The arrest of Abdullah al-Muhajir, also known as José Padilla (front page, June 11), opens up another frightening vista, this one on our doorstep. Apparently, Mr. Padilla, who started his career as a "mere" Chicago gang member, was radicalized into terror while serving time in prison. Multiply him by the prison population nationwide, and you have a fertile field for potential terrorists. Maybe Al Qaeda doesn't need Afghanistan after all; our prison system may do just as well. And that is scary. Bettie L. Roberts, Houston, June 11, 2002. ("Jitters in America" 8)

Roberts' discussion of Padilla's gang history, imprisonment, and alleged terrorist activity reiterates a causal relationship between each time-bound state of Padilla's life, and then extrapolates that to all inmates housed in U.S. prisons. Her narrative of terror is similar to Ashcroft's assertions and the stories presented in the media, but unlike those stories, she makes the links between Padilla's past and present explicit, and makes the connection between Padilla and "the prison population" clear as well. Roberts's letter demonstrates how the brands present in articles seeking to understand Padilla's present behavior by looking to his past not only work as a means to explain Padilla, but also as a means to define "the terrorist" writ large.

RACIAL PROFILING: DEFINING ENEMY COMBATANTS

The media's characterization of the Padilla case as an opposition between rights and safety revealed just how skewed the branding of terror had become. Padilla's case began to show how the branding of protection could not be squared with the branding of terror because not all citizens could be protected and not all terrorists were non-citizens. Instead of terrorists being discernable others who were outside the nation-state, as discussed in chapter three, Padilla's case situated terror inside the borders of the nation. And in doing so, the case called upon the same racist and colonial meanings attached to the brands of citizen and immigrant, discussed in chapter two. His case demonstrated how a Latino youth with a history of gang affiliation was seen as a threat to the U.S. family throughout his life. Instead of focusing on his citizenship status or his identity, the Padilla case constructed the man as an outsider, or worse a threat, and little else. By making his ethnic history visible, the rhetoric surrounding the detainment of Padilla began to disassemble the assemblage of the terrorist so that the colonial and racist legacies that underpinned it could be seen. As Horace Campbell points out, "The racial profiling and targeting of suspected terrorists in the United States brings the ideas and organization of yesterday's racial oppression in line with new technologies and the contemporary eugenics movement" (cited in Puar 145).

Padilla's case illuminated the relevant distinctions pertaining to race, religion, and legal designation under the Patriot Act. These distinctions, and their consequences for understanding the incommensurability of the rhetoric of protection and terror will be discussed in greater detail below. Suffice to say, in the media Padilla began to represent the necessity of governmental intervention, the removal of rights in the name of safety, the consequences of torture, and the loss of a truly free citizenry.

In his *New York Times* article "In Terror Cases, Administration Sets Own Rules," Adam Liptak discusses how the U.S. executive branch is using "enemy combatant"—a classification formerly employed during wartime on foreign soil—as a way to detain suspected terrorists without due process. Much like the work of ICE allows for immigrants to be regulated without the establishment of national laws, the government is now using military law to police and provide protection to the nation and its citizens without changing statutes or actual laws. Liptak states:

> The mere possibility of being named an enemy combatant, coupled with the difficulty of divining the standards the administration uses in choosing whom to call one, can affect the decisions of defendants in criminal plea negotiations. "In the case of John Walker Lindh," said his lawyer, James J. Brosnahan, "there was a suggestion that even if we got an acquittal that he could be declared an unlawful combatant, that he could be a Padilla." (Liptak 11)

According to Liptak, Lindh's lawyer worked out a bargain to prevent his client, a citizen just like Padilla, from becoming "a Padilla." Brosnahan knew the dangers of being named an enemy combatant under the current administration, and he did what he could to make sure that Lindh did not face those charges. Not only does this passage demonstrate the legal caution surrounding "enemy combatant status," which is due to the fact that our justice system has no control over said criminals. But it also uses Padilla as a stand-in for the term "enemy combatant." Here is a demonstration of how Padilla once again becomes a brand, a term of the debate.

But what is overlooked in Liptak's argument are the military and legal histories surrounding the term "enemy combatant." Prior to 9/11, an enemy combatant was deemed either lawful or unlawful, but in either case was a prisoner of war. Because this status was attached to prisoners of war, it was not often exercised against citizens of the imprisoning country; however, if it was, there were very stringent guidelines for its application, one being that the citizen must have been giving aid or assistance to the *government* of another warring nation. In other words, both lawful and unlawful enemy combatants were most often so designated owing to their connections with one or another nation-state during wartime.

William Haynes, in his memo reprinted on the *Council on Foreign Relations*, articulates the history of the designation "enemy combatant." He even cites the original military law in which the stipulations for citizen "enemy combatants" are defined. He writes:

> An "enemy combatant" is an individual who, under the laws and customs of war, may be detained for the duration of an armed conflict. In the current conflict with al-Qaeda and the Taliban, the term includes a member, agent, or associate of al-Qaeda or the Taliban. In applying this definition, the United States government has acted consistently with the observation of the Supreme Court of the United States in Ex parte Quirin, 317 U.S. 1, 37-38 (1942): "Citizens who associate themselves with the military arm of the enemy government, and with its aid, guidance and direction enter this country bent on hostile acts are enemy belligerents within the meaning of the Hague Convention and the law of war." (Haynes "Enemy")

His article serves to underline the legalities of "enemy combatants" within the context of post–9/11 governmental decisions. Because the Bush administration has defined the United States as existing in a state of war, those labeled enemy combatants in the fight against terror were so labeled legitimately.

Haynes goes on explaining that citizens deemed terrorists are designated as enemy combatants, and that this designation does not require them to be treated under the stipulations of the Geneva Convention. Therefore, their detainment and treatment therein is not legislated quite as stringently. Haynes states:

> The President has determined that al-Qaeda members are unlawful combatants because (among other reasons) they are members of a non-state actor terrorist group that does not receive the protections of the Third Geneva Convention. He additionally determined that the Taliban detainees are unlawful combatants because they do not satisfy the criteria for POW status set out in Article 4 of the Third Geneva Convention. Although the President's determination on this issue is final, courts have concurred with his determination. (Haynes "Enemy")

This passage demonstrates that the President's actions, although not determined by, have been supported by the judicial system. But more importantly it demonstrates that "enemy combatant" status is determined by removing the attachment to any given nation-state. Once deemed an enemy combatant, a citizen loses all his/her claim to national identity. And this loss allows citizens to be treated as war criminals on foreign soil.

Their non-state status makes them an exception, and therefore, they do not have to be tried as a foreign national—whether he/she is an enemy combatant or not.

Padilla's status as a U.S. citizen would seem to complicate the brand of enemy combatant, but as Hayes clarifies above, enemy combatant status allows for citizens to be stripped of those rights. What Hayes's article illuminates is that the Bush administration is not accusing Padilla of a military crime, but they are accusing him of being a non-state actor even though he is born of this country and a legal member of this nation-state. The state's accusation, through its adherence to military law, has essentially removed Padilla's citizenship rights due to his alleged behavior and affiliation with terrorist organizations. Because he is not being tried as a criminal within the judicial system, Padilla, as an enemy combatant, requires no due process, and so, he may be considered guilty until proven innocent. And all his rights as a citizen of the United States are suspended indefinitely—or as long as we are at war with terror.

But the "war on terror" is not a war between specific countries or legal entities. It is not a "war" in the classic sense. Therefore, Padilla's charges as an "enemy combatant" hold different material consequences than those of a traitor. First of all, one can be a traitor without the backdrop of war, and once named as such, there are strict rules as to the due process involved with being convicted of treason. The U.S. Constitution, article III, section 3 states:

> Treason against the United States, shall consist only in levying War against them, or in adhering to their Enemies, giving them Aid and Comfort. No Person shall be convicted of Treason unless on the Testimony of two Witnesses to the same overt Act, or on Confession in open Court.
> The Congress shall have Power to declare the Punishment of Treason, but no Attainder of Treason shall work Corruption of Blood, or Forfeiture except during the Life of the Person attainted. (U.S. Const. art III. sec. 3)

There are two major differences between the status of "enemy combatant" and "traitor." The first is that the traitor can be named outside of a context of war, and can only be convicted if there is testimony from two witnesses in open court. Secondly, only Congress can declare punishment for treason, and that is only after a trial and a conviction. A traitor, then, retains their rights as a citizen, and even though they are not necessarily tried in criminal court, they are entitled to due process.

Padilla's criminal charges also led to questions of treatment while in custody. An article in the *Santa Barbara Independent* discusses how language leads to material consequence for Padilla. However, through the rhetoric of Olivia Kienzel it becomes apparent that even those who are invested in exposing the injustice of the Padilla case still do not speak of

him as an individual with agency. Instead, he becomes not al-Qaeda's
pawn, but rather one of the U.S. government. Kienzel states:

> Right now, the case of José Padilla serves as a reminder that our execu-
> tive branch still likes to extend its reach into criminal justice in times of
> perceived threats from outsiders. . . . Padilla was arrested in this coun-
> try. He is also an American citizen. However, the President used his
> position as commander-in-chief of the armed forces to designate Padil-
> la an "enemy combatant" and move his trial to a military tribunal.
> (Kienzel 19)

Kienzel, like many independent and liberal journalists, is exposing the
inequity inherent in the Padilla case. Much like the development of ICE
and the erosion of civil liberties created by the Patriot Act, the branding
of Padilla as an enemy combatant not only serves a rhetorical function. It
is fraught with material consequences for Padilla.

One such consequence was his time spent in detainment before being
offered a trial. Padilla was detained in Chicago on a material witness
warrant and named an enemy combatant, an enemy belligerent, and a
serious threat. He was not held in a federal jail, but instead was sent to a
military compound where he was denied due process and access to a
lawyer. At the time of his arrest, there was no hard evidence to justify
holding Padilla for over a year. Then in 2003, a typed form with his
Muslim name that may have had his fingerprints on the document was
leaked to the press. Nevertheless Padilla was held in a military brig without access to counsel until 2006, and he was not officially tried and convicted until 2007. He was convicted not of terrorism, having a dirty
bomb, or being a member of al-Qaeda. Instead, he was convicted of aid-
ing terrorism through monetary support.

Once again, I turn to Jasbir Puar, whose analysis of post–9/11 terrorist
images discusses how the terrorist assemblage is deeply connected to
past histories of colonization, racialization, and sexualization of bodies
throughout the history of the United States. Many of the traits that are
associated with the terrorist were once tied to particular social groups *and*
removed from those bodies and presented as behaviors and/or traits. For
her, these moves create new ways of understanding representation and
identity within the context of patriotism in a post–9/11 world. Puar recognizes that the assemblage is a means of policing the nation-state and
protecting citizens from those who pose a threat. But even more than the
process of assemblage itself, Puar sees the terms of description of the
terrorist shifting as the war of terror wages on. It is caused in part by the
way context shifts the language. Puar states:

> This is a shift from "unstable generalizations" (race, ethnicity, gender,
> as well as what people do: arrived late at night, arrived early, arrived in
> the afternoon; first to deplane, last to deplane, deplaned in the middle)
> to "stable generalizations": how people seem. A patrolling of affect

changes the terms of "what kind of person" would be a terrorist or smuggler, recognizing that the terrorist (terrorist is brown versus terrorist is unrecognizable) could look like anyone and *do* just like everyone else, but might *seem* something else. (Puar 197)

Padilla then becomes a new kind of enemy, one that the state must discipline and contain outside the "normal" structures, but who is described by recognizable language—a threat that is at once visible and invisible. Padilla is described as a "stable generalization, one whose behavior seems as if it is that of a terrorist," and all the media coverage works to prove that supposition.

Padilla is described as a member of a social, ethnic, racial, and religious group which predisposes him to certain behaviors. He seems as if he'd be a terrorist because he was a gang member who turned to Islam. Padilla becomes both an individual and a member of a group, whose deeds make him both identifiable and anomalous. Within the branding of terror there is a shift from marking others (terrorists and threats) and citizens (Americans) by their appearance—or our assumptions about their appearance—to something far less visible—their behavior. Padilla, then, becomes the threat that is not identified by his appearance. He is not clearly a Muslim, but he converts to Islam. He is clearly a U.S. citizen, but he will not be tried as one. These contradictions create a threat that is pervasive, ever present, and deeply necessary to help shore up the nation-state in a time of distress. This fallacious reasoning makes the branding of terror necessarily vague and totalizing all at once.

Padilla's mother, Estella Ortega-Lebron, states, "He's a monster for the whole nation. They presented him as an al-Qaeda, as a Taliban, as a 'dirty bomber.' That's the government, but I know my son, and I know who he is" (Hirschkorn). She is attempting to redefine Padilla as a human being, not a pawn of state discourse and power. In a sense, he has been, like his mother claims, constructed as the monster-terrorist. But Padilla is not the quintessential monster-terrorist in the war on terror. In fact, he may just be one of the many U.S. nationals that have been collateral damage in the war on terror. His story, unfortunately, is emblematic in the sense that it was one of the first moments where the enemy combatant clause was enacted on a U.S. citizen, but it has not been the last. What Padilla gives us, then, is a better understanding of how branding is not only used to identify those who we recognize to be other. But it can also be used to create others when the situation warrants it. Padilla, then, is a much graver brand than those previously discussed in the book because he demonstrates how not even citizenship can prevent one's body from being branded. The U.S. government will do what it needs to solidify itself, even if it means putting its citizens in harms way. But in order to mask this reality, the U.S. government uses bodies like Padilla and bin Laden to justify its actions by associating terror with specific colonial and racialized histories. Thus, it is never about protecting *only* the nation-state. It is about protecting us all from the terrors that lurk everywhere.

OSAMA BIN LADEN: THE FACE OF A MOVEMENT

Shortly after the fall of the twin towers on September 11, 2001, President George W. Bush vowed to end terrorism across the globe. As I discussed in chapter three, his vows to quell terrorism in all of its forms were a rallying cry, but also a means of stirring the fear already growing inside of a wounded U.S. public. Bush's speeches, legislation, and agenda post–9/11 all focused on the United States's strength and resolve—both essential characteristics in the fight against terror. Yet, as I and several other scholars have discussed, terrorism is a faceless threat. Therefore, Bush branded the leader of al-Qaeda—Osama bin Laden—as the face of the terrorist effort against the United States. And Osama bin Laden became the face of terrorism across the globe.

Of course it did not help that Osama bin Laden made and distributed video tapes wherein he, as the leader of al-Qaeda, claimed responsibility for the 9/11 attacks. I want to be clear here, however. He himself was not laying claim to the attacks. Instead, he was representing al-Qaeda as their leader, and in that position claiming responsibility for the attacks. It may seem as if that is a minor difference, but for the purposes of this book, his own video admission reifies his position as a representation or brand. Even bin Laden reified his own brand through his videoed messages to the United States. As the war on terror continued, he recognized how his body was branded, and thus forwarded the brand himself as a means to suture his image with that of al-Qaeda. Again, he is not Osama bin Laden the individual. Instead, he is Osama bin Laden, representative of al-Qaeda. This difference, however, was never articulated, and because he had positioned himself as the leader and spokesperson of the cause, Osama bin Laden easily became *the* subject responsible for the attacks of 9/11 in the U.S. cultural imaginary regardless of the material realities of who actually orchestrated the crimes.[5]

The branding of Osama bin Laden as *the* terrorist created a world-wide, decade long manhunt wherein bin Laden was the supreme prize. This is in contradistinction from the vague, invisible threat of terror discussed at length in chapter three. But as I stated above, this contradiction is at the very heart of the branding of terror and the terrorist. They are an identifiable other all the while being an ephemeral, invisible threat that can never be located or expunged. For over a decade, as the war on terror developed into a global obsession, Osama bin Laden became both invisible—an elusive individual who evaded capture—and hypervisible—a household brand that represented all "terrorism" was.

Henry Louis Gates, Jr. has discussed the co-constitutive concepts of invisibility and hypervisibility in connection to black male identity in the United States. He argues that black men are invisible within traditional masculine and capitalist narratives of success and progress. But they are also hypervisible in narratives of crime and threat. Therefore a black man is both invisible in the traditional roles of capitalism (worker, consumer), but hypervisible in those roles that threaten capitalism (poor, thief) (Gates "The Signifying Monkey"). It is the "both/and" social construction of identity which influences how black men are allowed to function within American society. There are some exceptions, of course, and those exceptions can be seen in discussions of "the talented tenth" or other professional individuals. However, the arrest of Gates while entering his own home through a window in Cambridge, MA, tells just how functional the dichotomy of hypervisibility and invisibility still is. Although Gates may be an upstanding black professional when walking the halls of Harvard University, when climbing in a window in an affluent neighborhood in Cambridge, he is seen as just another black thug.

In the case of bin Laden, we can see how hypervisibility and invisibility begin to collapse into one another. He is a hypervisible terrorist who has become branded as *the* central mastermind of the September 11th attacks (even though that has now been proven through research to not be accurate). But as Puar and Rai show, a terrorist by nature is an invisible threat, one that cannot be located or fully identified. Therein lies the inherent contradiction of bin Laden's hypervisibility. He is hypervisible as an invisible brand.

Yet, there was an identifiable man named Osama bin Laden who once led al-Qaeda and claimed responsibility for the September 11th attacks. Therefore, as much as he has been rhetorically reduced to a brand and made into an invisible threat, he is also a very visible and material human. He *was* a person. He just could not be found. And his elusiveness allowed for the materiality of his body and humanity to quickly become just as invisible as his brand. And even when he was found, he was killed without images of his body—dead or alive—circulating. Without an image of bin Laden as a person, analogous to the images of the captured Saddam Hussein, there was nothing to remind us of his humanity.

When Saddam Hussein was found in a spider-hole, in tattered clothes, it was globally televised. During the broadcasts, one of the central memes under discussion was how small, dirty, and broken he looked. He no longer looked like the powerful dictator who had to be forcibly removed by the Coalition Forces. Instead, he appeared older, weaker. And he appeared this way to the billions of people across the globe watching his capture in real time. The juxtaposition of the litany of his crimes being discussed over an image of an unarmed, elderly, unwashed man created cognitive dissonance for the viewers and news reporters witnessing the scene. It is my contention that it was difficult to reconcile Saddam Husse-

in the man with the brand of Saddam Hussein the dictator we had all
been coached to hate.

The juxtaposition of man and brand continued throughout his trial,
but by then the media asserted it was merely a ploy by his defense to
make the "mass murderer" seem more sympathetic. That may be the
case, but I would argue that the media, like the voters of Kansas I discuss
in chapter one, long for a simple narrative. And reconciling the man with
the brand does not provide a simple narrative. Instead, it creates questions about humanity, representation, and materiality. These are not stories the neoliberal media sees fit to print, or so it seems.

So in the case of Osama bin Laden, it was acceptable that his real
image could not be found. In fact, it was advantageous. That way, the
brand could take over, and he was allowed to become the über-terrorist
of our times. Without a confrontation with his body, bin Laden, even in
the odd video message, was allowed to remain de-materialized: a bogeyman who was always primed and ready to come knocking at our door—
or worse, knocking down our buildings. That was until May 2, 2011. That
was the day the material body of Osama bin Laden confronted the brand
of Osama bin Laden, creating vast confusion in the U.S. media and
abroad.

THE ASSASSINATION OF OSAMA BIN LADEN BY THE COWARD U.S. PROTECTIONISM

On that date a covert team of military elite fighting forces landed in
Northeast Pakistan and raided a compound. In that compound was the
notorious Osama bin Laden and his family. According to the stories told
to the press, Osama bin Laden was killed along with several of his family
members. The early reports did not reveal much, but they did reveal that:

> There was a large shootout. The residents at the compound resisted.
> The total raid took 40 minutes. No Americans were killed in the mis-
> sion. . . . Officials said three adult men other than bin Laden were
> killed—one was believed to be bin Laden's son, the others couriers.
> One woman was killed when she was used as a human shield and two
> other women were also injured, the officials said. (Foxnews.com 1)

The story shocked the globe. No one expected bin Laden ever to be captured and brought to "justice." But much like his invisible brand, he was
not brought to a U.S., NATO, or even Pakistani court. Instead, there were
no cameras present, and the only notice of his death was given after the
fact. Therefore, the stories told became the only information about the
illusive man.

The description of the mission was reprinted in media outlets across
the globe, but by May 4, 2011, the story began to change. In particular,
there were conflicting reports and corrections about the death of bin La-

den's wife, her use as a human shield, and just how much enemy fire was actually deployed prior to the shooting of bin Laden. The secondary reports provided by White House officials began to contradict major events in the narrative of bin Laden's death. The only consistencies were that bin Laden was dead after U.S. troops invaded a remote compound in Northern Pakistan.

An example of the retractions or reframings came in a short but widely circulated piece from *Reuters* New York. It stated the following:

> A woman killed during the raid of Osama bin Laden's compound in Pakistan was not his wife and was not used as a human shield by the al Qaeda leader before his death, a U.S. official said on Monday, correcting an earlier description. John Brennan, President Barack Obama's top counter-terrorism advisor, told reporters earlier that the slain woman had been one of bin Laden's wives and had been used—perhaps voluntarily—as a shield during the firefight. However, a different White House official said that account had turned out not to be the case. Bin Laden's wife was injured but not killed in the assault. U.S. officials have said a small U.S. strike team, dropped by helicopter to bin Laden's hide-out near the Pakistani capital of Islamabad under cover of night, shot the al Qaeda leader dead with bullets to the chest and head. He did not return fire. (Reuters.com)

The representation of bin Laden's death here is quite different than the initial reports of a "large shootout" and a "resistant compound" where women were used as "human shields." Instead, this report describes a surprise attack where those inside the compound were caught off guard, and the ensuing firefight was defensive. Furthermore, any death of women or children, those who are constructed as innocent and in need of protection as I discussed in chapter two, was collateral damage to the mission.[6]

These blatant contradictions in the state's and media's presentation of bin Laden's death were further complicated by the fact that his body was never displayed. Despite several internet memes, Twitter discussions, and online petitions, he was buried at sea out of respect to Muslim law. President Obama insisted that it was disrespectful to both bin Laden's mortal soul, as well as the billions of Muslims across the globe to desecrate his body with a public viewing. So even though there were segments of the population who deemed him "without rights even in death" because of his murderous past, bin Laden's body was sent to sea without any media images or circulating visual confirmation.

Both the Associated Press and Judicial Watch, a conservative watchdog group, submitted Freedom of Information Act requests for the release of photos of the raid of bin Laden's compound, his dead body, and his burial at sea. The U.S. Justice Department has continuously denied those requests citing national security and the continued safety of U.S.

citizens at home and abroad. In fact, an *Al Jazeera* article from September 28, 2011 states:

> Images were taken of bin Laden's body at the Abbottabad compound, where he was killed by a Navy SEAL team, and during his burial at sea from the USS *Carl Vinson,* John Bennett, director of the CIA's National Clandestine Service said. "The public release of the responsive records would provide terrorist groups and other entities hostile to the United States with information to create propaganda," Bennett wrote, "which, in turn, could be used to recruit, raise funds, inflame tensions, or rally support for causes and actions that reasonably could be expected to result in exceptionally grave damage to both the national defense and foreign relations of the United States." ("U.S. Tries" 1)

The release of the photos, according to Bennett, is a matter of national security because it could stimulate further terrorist action across the globe. It could be seen as disrespectful to the dead, or it could be seen as a challenge to those terrorists who view bin Laden as a leader of terrorist activity. Either way, the U.S. government continues to refuse requests to release photos of bin Laden's killing and burial.

Respecting bin Laden's dead body was enfolded into the United States's rhetoric that killing bin Laden was not an affront to the Muslim world, but rather a blow to the war on terror, which effects everyone across the globe. As the *New York Times* reports:

> The president was careful to add that, as Mr. Bush did during his presidency, the United States is not at war with Islam. "Bin Laden was not a Muslim leader; he was a mass murderer of Muslims," Mr. Obama said. "Indeed, Al Qaeda has slaughtered scores of Muslims in many countries, including our own. So his demise should be welcomed by all who believe in peace and human dignity." (Baker et al. 5)

To insure that the United States was viewed as being among those who value peace and human dignity, even though they are involved in two seemingly never ending wars in the Muslim world and had just killed several "innocent women and children" as collateral damage in their mission to kill bin Laden, they gave the dead the dignity they did not in life. But doing this also allowed the United States to control the brand of bin Laden in ways they could not control the brand of Saddam Hussein.

By killing him in a possible "shootout," and then not allowing his body to be seen, the United States not only avoids a complicated international trial, but they also avoid the contradictory images of a disempowered captured leader presented to the world. Those contradictory and "messy" images do not allow for the brand of bin Laden to maintain its power as the über-terrorist, a brand which propels the nation-state's neoliberal identificatory capacities. Instead, as I argue happened with the Hussein capture in the spider-hole, those images create a dissonance so strong between the brand and the man, that the brand begins to lose its effectiveness.

In bin Laden's case, the brand needed to maintain its power because even in death, bin Laden was used to forward our fears about terror. Many within the U.S. military even noted that although bin Laden's death was symbolically significant, it does not signify the end of the war on terror. According to Al Jazeera.net:

> Mark Kimmit, a U.S. military analyst, said bin Laden's death "was not the end of terrorism, but an end of a chapter. Capturing or killing bin Laden has more iconic value. It will have symbolic value, because it has been a number of years since bin Laden has exercised day-to-day control over operations. We still have an al-Qaeda threat out there and that will be there for a number of years," he said. (*Al Jazeera* 2)

Even the recognition that bin Laden's death is little more that symbolic in the material context of terrorism does not free it from the branding of terror seen over the past ten years. Within this single quote bin Laden is assembled with ongoing threats from al-Qaeda and other terrorist threats. So even in death, his brand is used to evoke the war on terror. There is no significant material change to the way he is used in the media. The only significant change is that the man himself is dead.

No longer is bin Laden the solitary nexus of terror, but instead, he becomes a piece of an assemblage of terror wherein his characteristics are shifted onto other potential invisible terrorist plots. And as I discussed more fully in chapter three, the assembling of brands does not allow for material connections to be made. Instead it creates ephemeral connections based on the commodification of the historical and ideological characteristics of the brands being assembled. The U.S. government may have granted "dignity" to the body of the man Osama bin Laden, but the brand is still as undignified as ever. And the U.S. government and media are continuing to use the brand of bin Laden, even in death, to forward the agenda of the war on terror.

By assembling new branded threats rhetorically, the U.S. government and media are using bin Laden as a form of bare life both rhetorically and materially. He was both expelled through death, and also expelled as a brand, but not before his brand is transferred onto viable new threats. According to Sen. John Kerry:

> The killing of Osama bin Laden closes an important chapter in our war against extremists who kill innocent people around the world. We are a nation of peace and laws, and people everywhere should understand that our 10-year manhunt was in search of justice, not revenge. Terrorists everywhere must never doubt that the United States will hunt them down no matter where they are, no matter how long it takes. (Wilson et al. 7)

Just as the chapter is closed, it is reopened with a warning that those who might follow in bin Laden's footsteps will face the consequences brought forth by the U.S. nation-state. Bin Laden may be seen as a historical footnote, but his branded legacy is used to forward the United States's image as a terror fighting nation. Even prior to this "win," the United States asserted that they were focused and successful in the war on terror across the globe. The death of bin Laden in the rhetoric of the U.S. nation-state just solidifies that position. Yet, it also solidifies the need to continue fighting terror. Because as each of these government and media representatives are quick to note, we may have won this battle, but the war is far from over.

BARE LIFE: THE NEOLIBERAL NATION-STATE IS NEITHER GONE NOR FORGOTTEN

Both the brands of Padilla and bin Laden serve as reminders in a post–9/11 world that the United States is not safe either inside or outside its borders. I discuss the definition of borders through branding of an inside and outside at length in chapter two, but these two cases push the limits of branding. Instead of merely becoming representations of what we must contain or expel, they become casualties of the nation-state's fear of its own loss of power. As argued throughout this book, the evolving practices of neoliberal capital have in turn produced a shift in liberal governmentality. And although these shifts appear to have been wholly embraced by the global West, there are nonetheless affective traces of the need to govern and protect. The cases of Padilla and bin Laden represent the material consequences of those affective desires. To return to Agamben, he discusses the paradox in democratic states wherein political life (*bios*) and "natural biological life" (*zoê*) become separated, and political life (or citizenship and all the rights therewith) becomes the defining factor of the value of life in a democratic state. Although this may seem as if it is a sensible definition within political and legal realms, Agamben points out that instead of the term *citizenship* or *political life* circulating as representative of one's value, the term *life* (which often is used uncritically—invoking the idea of "natural life") is used. This is where the disconnection between *bios* and *zoê* is made the most visible. The state must continually produce examples of the value (and nonvalue) of life in order to maintain its power over its people. However the state often conflates these terms, so that it is difficult to tell if the state is attempting to control our political or "natural" lives. In other words, according to Agamben, the state must produce examples wherein life must be spared or annihilated in order to demonstrate how the state can protect and serve its citizenry.

Agamben sees these moves as indicative of how democratic states are moving toward totalitarianism in order to maintain their national power in the face of global economic and migratory patterns. For Agamben, this shift is represented in how the state represents itself in connection to life, not law. He states: "Today politics knows no value (and, consequently, no nonvalue) other than life, and until the contradictions this fact implies are dissolved, Nazism and fascism—which transformed the decision on bare life into the supreme political principle—will remain stubbornly with us" (10). For Agamben, the most egregious misuse of power prompted by the democratic invocation of "life" is the development of "bare life" which serves to legitimize the state. According to Agamben, bare life is the "supreme political principle" because it demonstrates how sovereign states serve their citizenry by creating and managing exceptions. Bare life is the ultimate exception, and it is deeply tied to life or the loss thereof. For Agamben, bare life becomes the ultimate example of how democratic states have stumbled over the separation of political and natural life, and this separation will ultimately lead them to totalitarianism or fascism.

The branding of Padilla as an "enemy combatant" and bin Laden as *the* "terrorist" serves to bring into stark relief the limits of the state's ability to protect its citizenry through democratic ideals and principles. In both instances, as Agamben shows, there are deep contradictions in juridical procedure and in how the representative stories are told. One might think it is just because the news media is not getting the information fast enough or that the government is in control of the story.[7] However, I argue that the discrepancies both legally and media-wise arise from the contradictions inherent when brands come into contact with material circumstances. In other words, the incarceration and torture of Padilla and the death of bin Laden are both material circumstances that cannot be completely evacuated of their histories, contexts, or bodies. In other words, they cannot be fully branded.

These are the contradictions Agamben sees at work in the presence of bare life, particularly as liberal governmentality faces decline in the age of neoliberalism. Even though the nation-state is giving more and more power to economic elites and corporate interests, in the face of security and protection of its borders it remains a viable organizing entity. Therefore, bare life is a site where those material contradictions are played out on the bodies of those who the nation deems inappropriate, expendable—the "other others" to return to Ahmed's language.

Bare life, then, is a site where the state overtakes life in the name of political life, all the while obliterating natural life in order to reaffirm state power. However, instead of presenting a vision of borderless power nodes and networks, bare life reveals the downside to diminishing sovereign borders—the reaffirmation of the nation-state through police and totalitarian political presence. Agamben sees "states of exception" and the response of "force of law" as the new terrain of sovereign power, and at the center of this change is bare life. He writes: "The particular 'force' of law consists in this capacity of law to maintain itself in relation to an exteriority. We shall give the name *relation of exception* to the extreme form of relation by which something is included solely through its exclusion" (18). *Homo sacer* is an exception that must be expelled in order to define the state. However, through its abandonment or expulsion it becomes a defining part of the state. Bare life must be expelled, stripped of its rights, but it still serves to define the state as that which must be abandoned, and thus it serves an integral function to the reestablishment of the "force of law."

Padilla can be seen as this kind of exception. He is stripped of his rights, but not sacrificed, for his crimes are too great to be granted sacrificial or regenerative properties. Instead, he is exiled to a military prison within the United States where he is still held, but not treated as a U.S. citizen. As an "enemy combatant" he works to define the limits of tolerance and the force of law which establishes the juridical boundaries of the nation-state. However, he cannot be expelled or deported because he is not a true outsider. José Padilla is bare life as described by Agamben.

Osama bin Laden is also this kind of exception. But he functions differently in the cultural imaginary. Although he is not a citizen of the United States, his deep ties and knowledge of U.S. affairs and his open judgment of them make him a vocal outsider—one who takes on the mantle of über-terrorist, the one who must be expelled for us to be safe. The nation-state must provide this safety as a means of recommitting itself toward democratic principles through some of the most undemocratic means imaginable. By expelling and branding bare life, the nation-state proves itself strong and resilient again. Even though it is known that bin Laden the man is no longer a threat, bin Laden the brand most certainly is. Therefore, he must be expunged and his life must be taken.

Bare life is the ultimate violence a sovereign power can commit against its citizenry in the name of its citizens. Instead of taking a life in order to protect, renew, and/or reestablish values or morality amongst the people, bare life serves to reestablish nothing but the power of the nation-state. And in its reestablishment, it takes the (political) life from one of its citizens and abandons that person as an exception to the rule of law, all the while using that exception to reassert sovereign force. "The very rights of man that once made sense as the presupposition of the rights of the citizen are not progressively separated from and used outside the context of citizenship, for the sake of the supposed representation and protection of a bare life that is more and more driven to the margins of the nation-states, ultimately to be recodified into a new national identity" (133). Agamben sees the margins as a site of developing identities; however, he does not assert this to be a necessarily positive development. It is from the margins that the sovereign state works to define itself through force, and although a new national identity may form from the margins, it is not necessarily exempt from the force of law, as Agamben has shown. Instead, Agamben calls for a progressive re-imagining of life wherein the life of the citizen possesses many of the same features as the life of a human both inside and outside the context of citizenship.

These are the arguments made in human rights discourse, as well as in independent presses throughout the Padilla case. Is it fair that when Padilla is stripped of his rights as a citizen he is also stripped of his human rights? Is it fair that non-citizens of the United States face different legal structures than those who possess naturalized or birthright citizenship? According to Agamben, it is not fair, but it makes sense within the development of modern democracy, and as such, the sovereign U.S. state post–9/11 is an inevitable development within the logic of democracy.

Padilla and bin Laden's narratives show how branding begins to break down when confronted with cases where humanity cannot be denied. The confusion surrounding the reports of their treatment and death, the evasions surrounding their whereabouts, and the lack of photographic evidence, all reveal that material bodies *must* be kept away from the brands that are created from them. If not, the brands will not provide the ameliorating affect they promise because they cannot escape the bodies they are branding.

Furthermore, the branding of bodies creates the spaces where citizens and humans become symbolic, and thus expendable without much thought. Instead of being humans who are detained without due process or killed without a fair trial, these men were tortured and killed without any thought about their humanity—until after the fact, or so it seems. But the ruptures in the media narratives surrounding each event reveal that brands don't always stick, and there is room to fight against them. The totalizing system of the neoliberal nation-state and its branding cannot contain and erase all humanity. The stories of José Padilla and Osama bin Laden reveal these schisms.

NOTES

1. The term "disappeared" refers to the political act of removing dissidents and citizens without warning or notice. This happened most notably in several Latin American dictatorships in the latter part of the twentieth century. Those who were disappeared were presumed to have been killed. However, their bodies were never found, nor were any details of their kidnappings and/or deaths given.

2. The examples below represent discussion of the Padilla case present in "liberal" and "conservative" presses from 2002 to 2007. Although these excerpts are taken from specific newspapers, they are more representative of media's construction of the "Padilla story" than of the specifics of the presses from which they come.

3. I use this term intentionally in order to allude to those who have been "disappeared" by dictatorships throughout Latin America. Many liberal presses presented this connection in terms of Padilla. This is a slippery connection that obviates the fact that everyone knew where Padilla was throughout his detainment, and those who have been "disappeared" in Latin America were not so fortunate.

4. I have included a Letter to the Editor here, not because it is indicative of liberal or conservative media discourse, but rather because it demonstrates how these discourses "stick" (to use Ahmed's term) and circulate throughout the social imaginary.

5. According to U.S. intelligence and the *9/11 Commission Report* the mastermind behind the planning and execution of the September 11th attacks was Khalid Sheikh Mohammed. Although bin Laden provided financial and intelligence support, he was not directly involved in the day-to-day planning and execution of the crime. Khalid Sheikh Mohammed was found in Afghanistan in March 2003. He confessed to his leading role in the 9/11 attacks in 2007, and was convicted of war crimes in 2008.

6. Also in fundamentalist Islamic law, hiding behind a woman in death ultimately disgraces both the woman's and the man's death. So if bin Laden had truly used his wife as a human shield, both of their deaths would be considered dishonorable per Muslim law.

7. This was one of the arguments for having embedded reporters in the Iraq invasion—the idea that a war abroad did not allow for "real time" information to be disseminated. However, as many scholars have discussed, the embedded reporters served less as a conduit for information, and more as a means for the military and government to control the media and thus the "story" of the military action.

FIVE

From Branding to Bodies

(Re)Assembling the Worker

BRANDING THE WORKER: LABOR IN NEOLIBERAL TIMES

Throughout *Branded Bodies* I have focused on the cleaving of affective value from material value as a technology of neoliberal governmentality. As discussed in chapter one, the branding of bodies in politics, working much the same as the branding of products in marketing, serves to create an image or link to an ideal lifestyle with which the consumer of the image—in this case the U.S. public—can identify. The bodies in question are no longer attached to their material histories or contexts. Instead, branding evacuates them from any signs of humanity, as shown in chapter four, and makes them an empty signifier that occludes governmental deregulation, corporate offshoring, and defunding of social services. It is through the use of particular branded bodies (such as immigrants and GLBT people), to signal threats which can rally an imaginary unified U.S. citizenry, that neoliberal governmentality can maintain its commitment to the logics of personal responsibility and the free market, thus continuing to cut support for public service programs because private companies and/or citizens will pick up the cost.

This trend has not only affected the lives of those who are labeled as threats—immigrant and GLBT bodies in particular—but it has also affected middle class and manufacturing sector workers across the United States. By trading a model of liberal governmentality—a model committed to protecting the rights and providing for the welfare of its citizens—for a neoliberal one—a model committed to protecting the free market and corporate interests—the U.S. government has insured that even workers who have kept their jobs are far less likely to receive adequate compensation, health benefits, or job security. Furthermore, the organizing and lobbying work of labor unions has been completely undercut through the implementation of right-to-work states,[1] such as Texas, Florida, and Louisiana, and adoption of pro-business legislation across the United States. Therefore, the category of "worker" is not as unifying or politically powerful as it once seemed because it neither carries the blanket national or statewide protections that work site enforcement once did. Furthermore, the lack of corporate and governmental support for workers has created a culture where identifying as "worker" is less desirable that identifying as an American or consumer.

Both the lack of corporate compensation and state support of workers' rights have created an environment where pride in work and/or identifying as a worker has been diminished. Instead, as discussed in chapter two, most people see themselves as private citizen consumers, and their jobs are the sites where they earn the money to purchase goods for their families and homes. In fact, in his first speech post–9/11, George W. Bush reminded the American public to "Go to work and spend." His reasoning was that if the U.S. economy continued to thrive, the "terrorists would not win." But for the purposes of this chapter, what is critical is the linking of work to consumption. It was not about getting U.S. workers back to work because they were needed for production of goods or because work was central to the U.S. citizen's identity. But instead, people needed to return to work so they could have the income to spend. In other words, they needed to work to consume; and if they consumed, they would be good patriots, thus good Americans.

The linking of work to consumption is another means of branding. It uses work not as a descriptor of the labor involved in the production of products, but instead to occlude those actions. Much like Bush's patriotic statement above, work is not central to conversations about what it means to identify as an American. It is an action U.S. patriots do so that they may consume, which is central to their identities. In other words, work becomes a mere stepping-stone to get to the real point of identification for Americans—consumption. When branded as such, all the rich international and domestic histories and material realities that connect "work" to the bodies of workers are effaced and those workers become a part of the neoliberal machine whose sole goal is to create and circulate surplus value. The worker, like the immigrant and GLBT body, however, is not a uniform category. There are some workers who are more prone to this branding than others. I return here to Grace Kyungwon Hong's work wherein she articulates how immigrant women of color are materially valuable to neoliberal capital—they do the work that produces the conditions under which capital can form, as discussed in chapter one. They are still seen as immigrants who are racially and nationally different, yet they are not seen as threats. Instead they are viewed as a necessary part of the system and are therefore coded as "others," to use Ahmed's term, who can be accepted into capital purely for their labor all the while being coded as different.

These differences in workers function both ideologically and materially. In chapter one, I discussed Texas's H.B. 2012 where certain immigrant workers were explicitly named as exceptions to a draconian anti-immigrant bill. By identifying employers who hired domestic service workers (such as nannies, gardeners, and housekeepers) as exempt to fine and imprisonment, the Texas legislature branded some immigrants as safe and others—the ones who worked outside the home—as threats. This differentiation marked immigrants, but also branded them as workers. The immigrants in the bill were marked as different, but by placing the exemption on their workplace status, it allowed Texas to see immigrant workers as bodies whose sole purpose was to serve the Texas economy. This evacuation of identity, context, and history brands work and defines it solely as a component of capital.

However, as described in chapter one, the immigrants, even as workers, were marked as different; and these differences did draw on material—although not complex—circumstances. Therefore, H.B. 2012 and its exception reveal a clash between the branding of bodies and the material reality of those bodies, in particular the locations in which they reside. Much like the examples of Osama bin Laden and José Padilla discussed in chapter four, the term worker offers an opportunity to examine how the material contexts and the brand come into contact and complicate one another. As shown in the Texas H.B. 2012 example, "worker" is not only a variegated category materially; it is also variegated when branded. For that reason, it is an important term with which to end *Branded Bodies* because "the worker" can both reveal the schisms present in neoliberal governmentality, and it can also provide a possibility for a re-imagining of rhetorical practice that can lead away from branding.

In chapter one, I discussed briefly how assemblage could be used not only to create new branded threats, but also new opportunities for resistance. By assembling events, material contexts, or even the histories of brands, a possibility for counter-narratives can arise because assemblages are not fixed. Manuel DeLanda argues that assemblages are about location and context. Their intelligibility requires "coding and decoding of meaning" (*New Philosophy of Society* 4). These codings and decodings are dependent on located understandings that are brought together to create the assemblage. Therefore, even though assemblages, as shown throughout this book, can be used to support dominant ideologies, assemblages can change; they can mutate; and they can resist dominant interpretations. Their mutability gives rise to the possibility of new assemblages wherein scholars and activists can create different identifications that work against the dehumanizing brands previously discussed in this book. This chapter, then, is a new kind of assemblage—one that, when placed contiguously with the other chapters of this book, should provide

a counter-narrative about the resistant possibilities of the assemblage itself. By creating new assemblages that bring together not brands, but
bodies and circumstances, assemblages can begin to rematerialize the
bodies that have been branded, thus creating a better understanding of
the material and cultural circumstances of immigration, GLBT action,
and U.S. neoliberal governmentality.

In this chapter through exploration of the brand "the worker," I will
show how immigrant and GLBT groups who are trying to gain rights
attempt to rebrand the term in the name of worker and human rights. It is
my contention, however, that rebranding is not enough. Re-assembling
"the worker" is what is needed. If the term is assembled the complex
material histories that undergird the brand can begin to re-materialize the
debates and people who are central to neoliberal capital. To demonstrate
the failure of resistant branding, this chapter will articulate how work
was branded through GLBT advocacy for the Equal Non-Discrimination
Act (ENDA) in 1996. Next, I will show how immigration rights activists'
attempt to assemble work with the brand of the family did not re-brand
the worker, but instead, affixed the white, heteronormative characteristics described in chapter two on to the worker. Finally, I will demonstrate
how the term *Si Se Puede!* invoked as a rallying cry during the 2008 May
Day protests, created an assemblage that provided a counter-narrative to
the brand worker. This chapter, then, serves to demonstrate a shift from
branding to the productive capacity of the assemblage to create rhetorical
action.[2]

WHY THE WORKER *WORKS*: THE PRIVATIZATION OF PUBLIC SERVICE

Since U.S. society has moved from a manufacturing model to one of
global exchange, individuals have become less connected to their position as workers. In fact, the gap between the professional and service
workers has grown, and the gap that was once occupied by livable factory or blue-collar union jobs is now filled with unemployment and seasonal service employment. As these shifts continue to respond to our neoliberal economic policies (NAFTA, CAFTA, and so on), labor in the United
States continues to become redefined as a site of struggle. A recent series
of *Mother Jones* articles discusses the "speed-up" of labor without monetary compensation at each job class from the professional (those with
advanced degrees) to service sector (those with a high school diploma or
less). Some of the examples discussed the increased speed with which
warehouse workers must box, load, and restock without breaks and over-
time compensation. In one particular example, a warehouse worker lived
in fear of losing his job if he could not do the work of the men who had
been fired due to downsizing in approximately two-thirds of the time.

Another example was of a corporate lawyer who, due to downsizing at her firm, doubled her caseload over one year's time, but received no raise nor additional time off. Instead, she was expected to increase her time at the office or lose her job.

The speed-up of labor across job classes demonstrates that all workers are, in their own contexts, facing similar pressures from capital. So even though capitalism has shifted since Marx's original call to organize labor—there is still something profoundly possible in the uniting of labor. It is because, as the *Mother Jones* article demonstrates (and I have given just two examples from the several well-articulated examples discussed in the article), capital exploits labor across all job classes. Neoliberal capital is particularly guilty of this exploitation because of its focus on excess and exchange. The processes and products of labor are completely disarticulated from the capitalist system currently in place. Therefore, workers are made to feel completely replaceable and dispensable. The more disposable workers become, the more anxious they feel. As I discussed in chapter one, this anxiety is often assuaged by branding bodies who then become a site for misplaced emotion. Those bodies, more often than not, are characterized as social and economic threats.

As discussed throughout the book, immigrants are framed as threats to the U.S. nation-state. Texas's H.B. 2012, articulated in chapter one, demonstrates that immigrants are not only threats if they are criminals, but they are threatening as workers as well. Thus, the search for illegal immigrants working in U.S. factories has become a priority of ICE, as well as local governments. The policing of immigrants through Worksite Enforcement is one of ICE's new fronts on the war on terror. It is designed to work with corporations in order to provide a streamlined process of reporting to ensure that illegal immigrants will eventually have nowhere to work due to strict enforcement at the workplace. ICE's Worksite Enforcement plan works to shift the burden of immigration enforcement onto corporations through a series of databases and potential fines. The development of this policy moves the bureaucratizing of immigration law, discussed in chapter three, into the private sector. Although ICE creates, oversees, and enables the program, the surveillance is performed by corporations and/or individual employers. Thus, the policing of immigration is effectively privatized. On the "Worksite Enforcement" information page of the ICE website, it clearly articulates the growing connection between this governmental agency and corporate interests. It states:

> ICE unveiled the ICE Mutual Agreement between Government and Employers (IMAGE) program in July 2006. ICE recognizes that the majority of employers in this country want to comply with the nation's immigration laws. Yet, every day employers are confronted with illegal aliens attempting to secure jobs through fraudulent means, including the use of counterfeit documents and stolen identities. ("Worksite" 3)

In addition to "recognizing" the desire of employers to "comply with immigration law," ICE's statement quickly blames the breakdown of this partnership on the immigrant workers and their criminal behavior. According to this statement, corporations and large-scale employers want to comply with governmental regulations, but they are prevented from doing so because of the immigrant worker's fraudulent use of "counterfeit documents and stolen identities." Therefore, if the system fails, and undocumented immigrants are hired, it is not because we have outsourced the work of a government agency to untrained civilians. It is because the immigrants are criminals who steal and use counterfeit documents. There is nothing in the bulletin that critiques the policing of criminals by private entities; instead it is made very clear that IMAGE has spent millions of dollars putting in place an employment tracking system that all employers throughout the United States can readily use. Therefore, if there are mistakes, it is because neither employers nor ICE can be expected to track individuals who use stolen papers. It is not the system, but rather the undocumented workers within it that are creating the problem.

Furthermore, in a recent *New York Times* article, it was discussed how immigrant raids provide jobs and income for private security companies. So not only are these raids re-criminalizing the brand of the worker through the immigrant, but they are also increasing economic gains of private U.S. corporations. Although the companies do not raid the worksites themselves, they provide the building, administration, and staffing of the detention facilities where the immigrants who are arrested during the raids stay for an indefinite amount of time. Although there have been several inquiries into the humane conditions of the facilities, there have been very few companies who have lost contracts in the face of filth, illness, or even detainee deaths. Instead, the number of immigrants housed in these private facilities continues to grow as ICE raids corporate, manufacturing, and agricultural work sites.

Immigrants as workers, then, function much the same as the brand of immigrant as "bandit" or "terrorist" because those brands have been assembled. As I discussed in chapter three, when brands are assembled, the characteristics of a given brand can affix to another brand without analogy or causality. In this case, the brand of the worker adopts the criminal brand of the immigrant because they are assembled together through discussions of worksite enforcement. Therefore, the immigrant worker is now a threat, even though they are a benefit to our economy through their own labor as well as the privatizing of their detainment.

In the case of immigrant worker raids, workers are branded in the name of capital. Like the branding described in chapters two and three, the brand of the worker may have resulted in material effects, but it still possesses no materiality. Instead, branding creates empty signifiers that do not allow for connections with materiality or humanity. Therefore, when resistant groups attempt to "rebrand," they are merely invoking a shell or image—not truly changing the terms of engagement.

WORKER AS MOBILIZED BODY: HOW GLBT BODIES BECAME WORKERS IN A POST-DOMA WORLD

In 1996, in an attempt to retain some of the rights that DOMA would inevitably take away, Democratic and GLBT activists worked to insure that the workplace would be free of discrimination based on sexual orientation. The Employment Non-Discrimination Act (ENDA) was drafted and put before a vote during the same congressional session as DOMA, and it was the hope that by protecting particular rights relating only to the workplace, the GLBT community and their supporters could cement a win that would help soften the blow struck by DOMA. Unfortunately, ENDA did not pass, and it still has not passed even though it has been brought before congress several times over the past ten years.[3]

The decision in 1996 to package ENDA with DOMA was a strategic one, and those who support GLBT justice were hopeful that by connecting GLBT rights to the workplace, they would be able to remove the moral and religious implications of the marriage debate, and talk about GLBT rights in the language of civil and labor rights. This shift, they hoped, would enable the GLBT community to preserve some of the legal rights that DOMA would erase in a way that tapped into America's sense of fairness and equality. The hope was that it would be a way to vote in protections for GLBT people without asking members of Congress to take a stand that would be construed as overtly pro-GLBT.[4]

Chris Bull writes about the decisions that went into writing and introducing ENDA in 1996. He states:

> Drafted in 1994, ENDA marked a historic shift in strategy for achieving gay civil rights. For the previous 20 years activists had sought general civil rights protection for gays. But in response to polls suggesting that voters are more likely to support specific job protections than broad safeguards, ENDA's sponsors focused only on workplace discrimination. The bill is worded so that it would prohibit sexual-orientation discrimination in workplaces with more than 15 employees; there are certain exemptions for religious organizations. (Bull 41)

Bull reminds us that part of the reason why ENDA was drafted was in response to poll numbers. So yes, it was an important step in protecting the GLBT community, but it was also an instrumental one. By placing the rights of the GLBT community on the same level of workers' rights, the advocates and authors of the bill were attempting to remove the stigmas of morality and sex and merely focus on the worker identity of the GLBT community. In other words, by suturing their civil rights to the workplace, ENDA became less about protecting GLBT bodies and more about protecting the rights of workers equally.[5]

Additionally, connecting the GLBT community to the notion of work is a way to enfold them into our capitalist economic system. As M. Jacqui Alexander has shown, one of the threats of the GLBT body is that theirs is a non-procreative body, and in that sense, they are not tied directly to capitalism in the ways that heterosexual bodies are (*Pedagogies of Crossing*). By branding GLBT people as workers, the authors of the legislation are making visible the ways in which GLBT bodies are always already implicated in capital, just as much as heterosexual ones. Furthermore, by insuring that GLBT people have rights to benefits for their families and partners, the bill recodes GLBT bodies as procreative ones, who then are also connected to capital through reproduction and consumption. ENDA represents a move to brand GLBT bodies as workers who have families, and thus deserve equal rights in the workplace. They *are* workers, family members, and citizens of the United States; therefore, they should be granted the same civil rights.

By changing the debate to one of civil rights, rather than family law, those who supported ENDA expected that it would pass with relative ease. After all, pairing it with DOMA insured that it would be the "least gay" of the gay rights issues before Congress. Unfortunately, Congress did not see this as "the lesser gay rights bill," and instead of passing ENDA at the same time as DOMA, they defeated the bill leaving no specific worker protections based on sexuality. But it was not a complete loss for the GLBT community. In the wake of ENDA's failure, there were more and more corporations and private companies who understood the importance of workplace non-discrimination, and began to provide domestic partner and family benefits for their GLBT employees.

The branding of the GLBT worker also reifies the branding of those bodies. Since the passage of DOMA, the federal government has not intervened into the rights of GLBT citizens, leaving it to individual states to determine their family structures and rights. Yet, as I will discuss at length later in the chapter, states have often refrained from making laws regarding workplace and/or insurance rights, leaving those decisions to individual corporations. So for GLBT workers neither the national nor state governments saw fit to regulate who could receive protection or benefits in the workplace. By placing the onus on individual corporations, the state (at both levels) essentially privatized certain civil and domestic rights. As such, they allowed corporations the power to define who was a family and who deserved workplace protection.

The GLBT worker, then, becomes a pawn in a marketing schema of corporate responsibility and image. Depending on who their stockholders or shareholders were, a corporation or business would decide how to regulate and treat their employees. For example, Apple Computers was one of the first companies to forward a non-discrimination policy and provide benefits for GLBT partners and family members. Apple has always branded themselves as progressive and forward thinking. In regard to the GLBT community, they provide partner benefits, a gender identity and expression policy, and company training for transgender and GLB issues. As a company, they believe that being progressive in their thinking and employment sectors allows for their success. However, they do not advocate for GLBT rights in any way, though they are seen as sympathetic and "good" to the community. The connection Apple draws between employees and corporate interest, and the line drawn between corporate interest and political activism, could be understood as Apple supporting GLBT bodies, but only in the neoliberal sense. GLBT bodies are respected and safe at work. But Apple is not engaged in changing larger attitudes or policies because it is not their job. Their company is the only site wherein they have a say.

In the case of Apple, GLBT workers did gain the material consequences of the corporate decisions to provide a fair and safe work environment. But they also became far more instrumental to the corporate brand than other workers in the company. In other words, these bodies were turned into brands so that their material needs and protections could be used to forward the corporate identity of their employer. Apple was able to look progressive during the early 1990s by providing workplace rights to GLBT workers. But Apple was never interested in extending those discussions beyond their corporate purview.[6] The GLBT workers' rights became a pawn in capital. Once again, workers are central to the forwarding of the capitalist project, although in a different context and different formation than Marx described in the nineteenth century. This is the corporatization of worker's rights, and it serves to make civil rights as much a "product" as cheap goods. Civil rights come under corporate control, and because corporations are legally required to turn a profit, if the rights in question are not profitable, they will not be offered. The branding of the GLBT body as worker is an attempt to gain solidarity across group affiliation and forge connections between the dominant culture and their seeming counter-culture. However, what this actually did was create a deep connection between labor and civil rights that could be commodified by corporations who see these trends as good business.

Instead of the U.S. government providing basic rights for GLBT workers, much like the ones that were outlined in the Civil Rights Act of 1964, they instead allowed these workers to be regulated by the very people who can exploit and/or ignore their rights—the employer. Additionally, without a law in place, who gets supported or exploited is not only determined by someone's group affiliation, but it is also dependent on the class of job they are performing. In other words, without governmental protections based on the brand of "the worker"—which crosses all classes—the workers who receive the benefits of a generous corporation are often workers who are part of the professional class, not the working class. Again, we see echoes of Hong's work wherein workers are no longer excluded from discussions of rights, but instead are categorized through race and gender so that particular work can be rewarded while others labor without support in the name of capital.

Class becomes implicated in GLBT rights through the worker as an organizing brand because the workers who are supported by corporations are the ones who are most valued in society—the professional, educated class. The rights and privileges of being a GLBT professional worker far outweigh those of being a GLBT service worker in the United States. Lisa Duggan claims that neoliberalism and the rise of homonationalism have allowed for a cleaving of class.[7] Echoing Hong's statement regarding immigrants, Duggan offers a critique of a tendency within activism to cling to a universal term, or what I would call a brand. Duggan challenges an attempted inclusivity that occludes many issues of race and class, as well as the imperial histories that designate certain GLBT bodies as more acceptable within the U.S. imaginary. An opinion piece run in 1997 in *The Advocate* extols the virtues of corporate America for stepping in to regulate what the government refused to. Tzivia Gover writes:

> For Love or Money: Despite the Hawaii ruling, the federal government still won't recognize gay marriage, leaving only corporate America to give us what's right; domestic-partner benefits. . . . The bottom line is this: Companies are finding that to be competitive they need to attract top talent, which includes gay and lesbian employees. "I used to think it was a cliché to say that people are our most important asset," says Randy Massengale, diversity manager at Microsoft. "But people are our only asset. It's important to keep our people happy and productive." (Gover 66)

Microsoft, a Fortune 500 company that employs educated professionals, understands that to attract "top talent" they need to put in place domestic partner benefits. Microsoft's sensitivity to the GLBT community's needs—which as we are reminded, were ignored by the government— allows them to provide an inclusive work environment for all, GLBT workers included. It is not as if Microsoft is giving special rights or treatment to their GLBT workers; they merely insure that those workers have equal rights in order to keep all their workers "happy and productive." After all, as Massengale states, "people are our only asset," and if those assets are not happy, the work at Microsoft would fail. Much like children in the rhetoric of ICE discussed in chapter three, workers may be people, but more importantly they are property of the company. Therefore, the company is just taking care of its property, not making any commentary on the rights of GLBT workers in general. After all, it is not Microsoft's job to intervene in civil rights. They are a corporation who must turn a profit, and they need "top talent" who are "happy and productive" to do that.

Because of the government's lack of intervention, GLBT workers face the same discriminatory practices that the government enforces around immigration. What is different is that the GLBT worker faces discrimination at the hands of the private sector, not the government itself. However, the government's lack of legislation surrounding work is a way to discriminate against this particular population through negation. In other words, by placing the discriminatory power in the private sector, the government can shift the responsibility for workers and civil rights to corporations, and thus not intervene in the discrimination against the GLBT community in the name of privatization.

This workplace discrimination is representative of the yoking of the neoliberal logics of personal responsibility and privatization. By allowing individual corporations to determine the rights and welfare of a segment of the U.S. population in the name of workers' rights—thus the private interests of the workplace, not the whole of the nation—the state is abdicating its role as liberal government, as discussed by Dean, et al. in chapter one. The U.S. government is placing the private needs of business at the center of governmental policy, precisely by *abjuring* policy as such. Inasmuch as this shift is justified, it is done so through an implicit appeal to the discourse of personal responsibility—whether individual or corporate. Instead of regulating the rights of all workers, the U.S. government permits only certain companies who see fit to provide benefits to do so, which means that only those workers deemed *valuable* will be granted workplace rights. The government allows for this in the name of neoliberal progress.

The lack of governmental attention to the needs of the GLBT community can be seen in the ENDA legislation itself. Granted, this legislation is particularly geared toward workplace policy, and because of that it is part of a long tradition of legislation focused on workers' rights and employer responsibilities. But unlike other laws in place that target the workplace, this law targets the individual worker, which allows the law to establish particular definitions of those who are protected by this law and those who are not. In other words, much like the Civil Rights Act of 1964 that becomes central to ENDA through citation, ENDA works as a corrective establishing a defined group of workers who need the government's protection. In other words, ENDA functions to create protections for GLBT workers with the assumption that these protections are already given to non-GLBT workers. ENDA, then, works to define workers' rights by using GLBT bodies as a "suspect class" in need of protection.

A suspect class, according to the Supreme Court, is any group of people who is subject to governmental discrimination. It was developed as part of the 14th Amendment's Equal Protection Clause, which stated: "all legal restrictions which curtail the civil rights of a single group are immediately suspect. That is not to say that all such restrictions are unconstitutional. It is to say that courts must subject them to the most rigid scrutiny. Pressing public necessity may sometimes justify the existence of such restrictions; racial antagonism never can" (14th Amendment). This clause has been invoked to insure governmental intervention to alleviate discrimination against citizens. In the case of ENDA, however, the government demonstrated that it would much rather allow corporations to regulate the treatment of GLBT bodies instead of the enforcing regulation itself. In response, GLBT activists invoked the Equal Protection Clause to force the government to intervene.

With ENDA, much like the earlier laws, petitioning the state ended up creating a space where the family and especially children are assumed to require protection. By placing the brand of the GLBT worker on the national stage, GLBT sexual practice instead became a focus of the conversation. I argue that this is due to the assemblage of brands which created an association between the worker, GLBT body, and predatory practices. Therefore, the presence of GLBT bodies, regardless of whether they were workers or not, became a site where heterosexual, monogamous sexual practice could be come normalized yet again. In the debates surrounding ENDA, it was the case of Jeffrey Dion Bruton, a heterosexual-identified teacher who had acted in "gay porn" movies that brought these assumptions of normative sexual practice and the discourse of protection into question. Patrick McCreery, in his article "Beyond Gay: 'Deviant' Sex and the Politics of the Workplace," argues that although ENDA seeks to protect GLBT workers, by seeking protection based on sexual orientation and not sexual practice, the bill reinforces a heteronormative workplace in which GLBT practices can still be grounds for dismissal and ostricization. [8] He sites the "nonprivate conduct" clause of the law as being far too conservative and creating a loophole that allows employers to normalize the sexual practices of their employees through threat of termination. [9] McCreery argues that this clause, coupled with the definitions of sexual orientation as homosexual, heterosexual, and bisexual put forth by ENDA, served to reinforce the heteronormativity of the workplace through legal means (41).

According to McCreery, the Bruton case allowed conservatives to launch an argument against ENDA in which the protection of children from homosexual and non-private sexual practices became one and the same. He states: "Whenever gay activists appear to be on the verge of achieving a major victory, such as the passage of ENDA, the antigay discourse of endangered child welfare becomes shrill" (42). This was the rhetoric that halted the passage of ENDA, even though by all accounts it was an extremely conservative attempt at gaining rights for the GLBT community.

What McCreery's article helps to reveal is the way in which the GLBT community *could not* be identified only as workers. Instead, they had to become workers who engage in particular sexual practices that could only be protected if they approximated the heteronormative standard of monogamous sex. Now the nonprivate conduct clause does not single out GLBT sexual practice, stating that the rules apply "uniformly to all" employees, and in doing so, this clause creates a space for all workers to be not merely workers, but sexual beings as well. In a liberal sense, this move to identify more facets of the lives of employees and citizens is a good move toward recognizing that we are not all comprised of isolated roles and identities. However, in this instance, the presence of the nonprivate conduct clause undermines the activist move to identify GLBT laborers not by their sexual practices, but instead by their roles as workers.

McCreery makes these connections as a means to argue for a more comprehensive bill that protects sexual practice for those of any and all sexual orientation, and he sees this as critical because of the deep connections between the workplace, the economy, and heteronormative sexuality. Much as Alexander argues about the heteronormativity of the family in the eyes of the state, McCreery sees the worker infused with similar normative histories and expectations (50); therefore, for McCreery, ENDA was ill conceived from the beginning because using the workplace as a site of GLBT rights is almost as futile and reifying as using state recognized marriage as a site for political struggle.

The worker, then, much like the family, is a brand that is deeply infused not only with economic and political histories, but with normative social and national histories as well. The attempt to rebrand "the worker" and draw only on the economic and political realities of that brand did not allow activists and those who may have supported them to fully challenge the heteronormative power structures and societal assumptions embedded in that brand. It is not that GLBT people failed to become identified as workers, but rather that attempting to identify with that brand in itself was a move that allowed the GLBT community to reinforce the heteronormativity of the state through the rhetoric in support of ENDA as well as the bill itself.

However, if the rhetoric of the worker feeds the systems which normalize the nation as heteronormative, why didn't ENDA pass? Much like McCreery's analysis shows us, even though the workplace seems as if it is an equalizing space, in the rhetoric of ENDA, those GLBT members within it will always be defined by their sexual orientation or practices. Thus, they can never be merely workers, even in the workplace. The GLBT body can approximate the normalizing definitions created by heteronormativity, but they will always be marked as different when they speak or act out in the interest of their own protection.

Again, we see the attempt to brand "the worker" by creating the same questions of legitimation versus disruption of normative values that we saw with those who are attempting to legalize gay marriage. Those who want protection from discrimination in the workplace, like those who seek the legal privileges and protections of marriage, have very legitimate and material reasons for seeking these protections; however, by allowing themselves to become associated with an already predetermined heteronormative institution and role, they are giving up any chance at disrupting the systems that oppress those who are different.

In her article "Is Kinship Always Already Heterosexual?" Judith Butler discusses how the homosexual attempt to be included in the concept of marriage is a necessary call for legitimation, but one that necessarily closes off the disruptive potential of the homosexual body. It is the tension between the embodied subject's material need for legitimation and the material potential of disruption that is of particular interest to Butler. She states, on the one hand:

> If you are not real (legitimized by the state), it can be hard to sustain yourselves over time. The sense of delegitimation can make it harder to sustain a bond, which is not real anyway, does not "exist," never had a chance to exist, and was never meant to exist. Hence the absence of state legitimation can emerge within the psyche as a pervasive, if not fatal, sense of self-doubt. (133)

And on the other hand:

> In making a bid to the state for recognition, we effectively restrict the domain of what will become recognizable as legitimate sexual arrangements, thus fortifying the state as the source for norms for recognition and eclipsing the other possibilities within civil society and cultural life. (134)

Butler does not seek to minimize the material reasons that make legitimation important to any citizen of the state. In fact she is careful to point out that the desire for legitimation ("being made real") is an embodied and material need which manifests itself as psychic pain and alienation in profound ways. Without state legitimation there are certain rights that are not given to couples which allow sexual relationships the comfort and connection necessary for development. (The example of the lesbian partner who cannot visit her lover in the hospital is a material manifestation of the exclusion caused through delegitimation.) In other words, to be recognized is of material consequence, and at times it seems that becoming legitimate in the state's terms may be a more immediate need than attempting to disrupt those terms as a nonintelligible body.

This tension between the material need to become legitimate (or to *be* in the state or *recognized* by the state) and the material capability to redefine the state in relation to the concept of kinship by allowing the body to remain a brand which is always becoming (not fixed or finished) is a tension worth considering. According to Butler, the association of kinship with a particular definition of family is a particular historicized phenomenon tied to the nation-state. The definition of kinship, which is a way of understanding a subject's relation to others and the social, has not always been tied to the model of the family. But at this political moment the family *is* the definition of kinship, and as such the notion of the family holds great weight in designating who is legitimized and who is not in the eyes of the state. Thus the state is interested in regulating the rights of the family or at least appearing to do so.

The worker, however, is not as important to the state because the brand "worker" does not provoke nearly as much fear or desire for protection as the brand family. Therefore, the state is willing to privatize the concerns of workers not only to support the economic interests of corporations, but also because the brand of the worker does not ideologically serve the state. The worker, then, is not as effective an organizing brand as the activists in support of ENDA had hoped. Much like the activists against DOMA found, it is a brand that is not solely about the material and economic consequences of work; but instead, "the worker" becomes a brand that reifies the nation-state through its invocation in neoliberal economic debates.

WORKER AS "GOOD" FAMILY: DEFINING CITIZENSHIP AND HUMANITY THROUGH WORK

The brand of "the worker" did not stop circulating with the failure of ENDA in 1996. In fact, it has been the central organizing brand within the immigrant rights movement, especially in response to H.R. 4437. Immigrant rights groups, as well as those groups who were invested in fair immigration reform, mobilized around May Day (the historic, and current in some parts of the world, day of worker solidarity).[10] It was an attempt, much like the attempt by the GLBT community who supported ENDA, to redefine immigrants as workers rather than foreigners, criminals, or threats to our American way of life. There was the hope that by creating new associations between immigrants and workers, more citizens could understand how immigration was economically necessary for the well-being of the country, as well as for the immigrants themselves.

What was seen in most of the liberal alternative presses was an attempt to build coalitions between groups from various political backgrounds through a common commitment to work. Monika Joshi in her report of the May Day 2006 protest in *India in New York* states the following: "It was a motley crowd of political, labor, religious and community leaders, blue-collar workers, and even young children brought by their working parents to City Hall in Newark, New Jersey, on May 1 to participate in a rally in support of the rights of immigrant workers and their families" (8). Joshi's description shows there are more than just immigrants who are fighting for immigrant rights. The mention of "blue-collar workers," "labor leaders," and "working parents" demonstrates that this is not merely a debate about immigration. Instead, it is a debate about labor, something everyone does. Additionally, there is mention of religious and community leaders who were marching in support of the cause, individuals who bring a sort of validity to the protest because of their commitment to moral and social good.

But the moral and social good was covered in Joshi's short description when she invoked the family. Within this one short sentence she mentions "working parents" and "immigrant workers *and their families*" (emphasis mine). Joshi moves easily from the brand of the worker to that of the family—linking them together quite seamlessly. This is not the first place in politics where the linking of "workers" and "families" has been made;[11] however, it is a telling move that even in the description of a protest that attempts to celebrate the "International Day of Work" there is the need to emphasize the idea that immigrants are families, too. It is not enough that they are workers; to truly connect and seem sympathetic to a larger audience who might not share their values, immigrants must also be members of families.

Disentangling the worker from the family is difficult when the family has been put at the center of U.S. capital through its deep connection to Protestantism.[12] In her critique of the progressive Left's use of *freedom* instead of *justice* as a term for organizing, Janet Jakobsen discusses the deep Protestant roots of the U.S. government. It is not about the religious beliefs of the president or majority party, but rather the whole of the government's secularism is based in Protestantism. Therefore terms such as community and justice fall flat, whereas terms such as liberty and freedom—terms connected to a sense of individuality and private property—resonate with the public ("Perverse Justice" 24). Jakobsen ultimately wishes to challenge these terms and reassert *justice* as central to organizing because it allows for a disruption of the normalizing and privatizing terms and associations that are typically forwarded in public debate.

Jakobsen's argument is compelling in that it reveals yet another set of historical and ideological ties between capitalism, bodies, and privatization. Her argument to move toward a more contextual understanding of terms used within public discourses is much the same as the work done throughout *Branded Bodies*. Her critique, much like the one in this chapter, discusses just how pervasive these terms are and how they cannot shift the dialogue just because the progressive Left forwards them. Instead, new terms and commitments to historical and economic realities must be made. Because without that awareness, no change will be achieved or illuminated through rhetoric, no matter the context.

For example, an anonymous contributor to *La Prensa San Diego* makes the link between family, work, and society more directly when she states: "We believe it is imperative that all people of good faith who value family, workers' rights and quality education should come together today to celebrate the economic social and cultural contributions of hard working immigrants in America" ("Yesterday" 4). Right here we see the rhetoric of Protestant and capitalist values through the branding of immigrants as "family (members) and hard workers." The connection between education and family seems to evoke the intimate public sphere discussed by Berlant in chapter two. However, the invocation of "hard working Americans" speaks to a rhetoric that is imbedded in the "American identity" as far back as the Protestant yeoman farmer of Thomas Jefferson.[13] The notion of the "hard-working American," much like the protection of the American family, is a central brand within cultural, economic, and political debates. By placing the immigrant at the center of an assemblage of hard work and family values, the anonymous contributor is reifying the connection between a Protestant work ethic and moral family behavior and positing that family values *and* hard work are synonymous with American-ness. Therefore, the immigrants described are branded as American through their family and work status.

But some of the most significant uses of the brand of the worker during the May Day campaign are not the links made to the family status of immigrants. Instead, it is the insistence that because of their commitment to family and hard work, immigrants are human beings. The linking of work to the values of the intimate public sphere, and those values to the condition of being human both seeks to legitimize immigrants and connect immigration debates to popular human rights discourses. It is through the discourse of human rights that NGOs and other activist groups can not only get their messages heard, but can also gain funding from transnational sources who are invested in the well-being of women and children.[14]

The rhetoric of human rights can be seen in the discussions surrounding the May Day events that connect directly to the slogan "No Human is Illegal." The slogan coined by the Immigrant Solidarity Group speaks directly to H.R. 4437, but it also attempts to decriminalize and humanize immigrants as well. This creates a space where American citizens and those leery of immigration reform should attempt to see immigrants not as legal categories, but rather as human beings with similar goals and values. In the *Colorado Springs Independent*, Cara DeGette quotes an immigrants rights leader: "'We are human beings. We have dreams, we want a shot at life. . . . We are working people who deserve to be treated as human beings. Immigrants have created this country, whether they have been Chinese or Russian or Polish,' Velez says. 'Of course, they pay taxes, buy products, and, for the most part, don't use up services'" (DeGette 8). What is notable in Velez's statement is not that it invokes the idea of human treatment for immigrants, nor that it connects directly to the historic formation of the United States through immigration, but rather that it attempts to point out the ways in which immigrants are performing the tasks of citizenship. According to Velez, immigrants pay taxes, buy products, and do not rely on social services—all traits of upstanding American citizenship.

Velez's claims about the ways in which immigrants are both human and citizenship-worthy speak directly to the demands put forth by the

Immigrant Solidarity Group. By attempting to tie human rights to the work of the citizen, and thus the work of the state, they create a debate about immigration that is not merely about status, paperwork, and racist assumptions. Instead they reveal a debate that is deeply rooted in the economic and political practices of neoliberal economics. They do not go so far as to discuss the transnational consequences of the globalized U.S. economy. Yet they do present demands that speak to the decline of the welfare state in the United States. They assert:

> We demand jobs at a livable wage to provide affordable housing, health care, childcare, education, and other vital social services. We demand a broad reconstruction program starting with New Orleans and the Gulf Coast and continuing throughout the country. We demand that this program be accomplished by hiring workers through direct government employment to rebuild housing, schools, hospitals, day care centers, and other vital projects. Fund the program by defunding all the wars. We Declare: No human being should ever be illegal! (Immigrant Solidarity Group)

By connecting work, jobs, social services and immigration together in opposition to the lack of viable reconstruction of the Gulf Coast and the funding of the War in Iraq, the Immigrant Solidarity Group (ISG) is attempting to show how immigration, like education, health care, and social services, is a matter of human rights—not a criminal event. The rhetoric they employ here creates an image of immigration that builds on the American ideals of compassion and justice, which are the connections attempted in almost all human rights discourses.[15] Therefore, when they get to the notion that no human is illegal, they are no longer merely implicating immigrants in this discussion. Instead, they are calling upon the audience to recognize that immigrants, workers, children, and citizens are all in need of the U.S. government's assistance. For the government to continue to turn its back on these communities is the real criminal act.

Here we see a shift from the branding of the immigrant as family, worker, or student to the immigrant as part of a larger economic and political system. Yes, immigrants are all of those brands, but those brands are part of a larger system of government and procedure that is failing. Therefore, the rhetoric of the ISG is not about the identity or branding of the immigrant. It is about assembling the myriad of brands the immigrant represents to expose the flaws in neoliberal governmentality. The ISG is asking for a return to some of the aspects of liberal governmentality—or at least the parts where citizens garnered protections from the government.

But herein lies the difficulty with the ISG's argument. The linking of human to citizen has not been an issue for the United States. Most citizens across the United States have *used* immigrants and GLBT bodies as brands to maintain an affective connection to their citizenship status as their rights have been stripped away. Therefore, for the ISG to attempt to connect to those who see themselves as citizens is a precarious argument. For most U.S. citizens, not all immigrants can be citizens, nor are all citizens threats—recall the discussion of Ahmed's other and other-others. So to unify the category of human-immigrant-citizen in the context of work functioned much the same as branding those categories in the end. For immigrants to be seen as workers—a vast and variegated category— then U.S. citizens may have to do the same. For them, there would need to be some education about immigration and work regulations, as well as their own position within capital. So in light of these impediments, re-branding is shown not to work. Instead, what must happen is a reassembling of the material and global conditions of the brand "worker." This is beginning to happen through discussions of unemployment, job loss, and economic recession.

WORKING AN ISSUE: THE WORKER AS TRANSNATIONAL ACTOR

Part of the failure of the brand of "the worker" is that in the United States there is no longer a deep historical attachment to our labor and unionizing history, which the ISG was clearly trying to summon. Without this history through which to read the organizing actions on May Day or post-DOMA, there are no associations for the brand of the worker other than what we are offered by the current government and the media. These models are so infused with capital and neoliberal logic(s) and technologies, they can never represent the truly disruptive connection between work, production, and the worker which a socialist framework permits. Instead, the worker is yet another brand unmoored from its historical and economic purpose, left to be assembled with the brands that are associated with it—family, hard worker, criminal. Once again, these metonymic chains create a brand that functions self-referentially in order to create meanings for a people who have been thoroughly dissociated from any meaningful concept of what a worker is.

In May 2008, the National Immigration Solidarity Network (NISN) published the pamphlet *May Day 2008 International Workers Day Mobilization to Support Immigrant Rights! Reports from Around the World*. At only forty pages with images, the PDF circulated on the NISN's listerv one week following the May Day (May 1st) protests. The pamphlet is multi-authored and serves as means to document the events of May Day 2008 from across the globe through photographs, eyewitness accounts, and media stories. Although the bulk of the entries are from the United States, there are entries from across Europe, China, and Japan as well.

Through its photos and descriptions of events the pamphlet documents the variety of foci, activists, and activities involved. The pamphlet does not make each protest look identical, and this is an important development in comparison to the descriptions of the 2006 May Day protests. Instead of attempting to redefine immigrants within the United States, the 2008 protest has opened up the possibility for different localities to join together for action as they see fit. This allows for the rhetoric surrounding the protest to shift. Instead of focusing on the movement from immigrant to worker or family, it allows for new rallying cries that represent many different histories, groups, and actions.

The Call to Organize present on the first page of the pamphlet lays out the expectations for the year's protest. It clearly focuses on the joining of particular localities with their own topics and styles of organization. The call states:

1. Multi-ethnic, Decentralized and Multi-topic mobilization: while everyone will pledge to support immigrant workers rights at May Day 2008, local groups can choose to include any other topics for their mobilizations: civil rights, anti-war, Katrina, labor rights, health care, and so on.

2. Decentralized Multi-Tactic May Day organizing: We will encourage everyone to organize their actions at May Day, but will let local groups to decide what they want to do at the day: march, boycott, strike, lunch action, vigil, community event, conference or congressional lobby day, and so on. Understanding the connections between our individual conditions of life and the lives of people everywhere in the world allows us to come together and organize across all borders. WE NEED to link the connections between: wars in Africa, South America, Asia, Iraq, Palestine & Korea with sweatshops in Asia as well as in Los Angeles, New York; international arms sales and WTO, FTAA, NAFTA & CAFTA with AIDS, hunger, child labors and child soliders; multinational corporations and economic exploitation with racism and poverty at home–then we can win the struggle. (2)

Within the call, we see an awareness of the economic, historical, and political similarities from which Chandra Talpade Mohanty and Valentine Moghadam believe strong coalition building can come (*Feminism Without Borders, Globalizing Women*). Instead of focusing on shifting one groups' brand (immigrant) to another (worker) the NISN is accounting for the varied nature within groups by avoiding the use of brands to name the types of protest and protesters. Instead, the NISN focuses on history and economic conditions and attempts to make connections between neoliberal policies and their consequences that affect workers and immigrants worldwide, as well as those affected by war across the globe. There is no assumption that one brand can cover the experiences of all. Instead, there is the recognition that the transnational economic and political pressures and networks of power create enough similarities between the specific oppressions of local groups that there can be common ground from which to organize.

Although this may seem as if it is a diffuse way of protesting, the focus on May Day and its history both within the United States and internationally is cited as the reason for the success of the multi-strategy coalition. It is not assumed that this history is known. In fact, just one page after the call to action, there is an account of the San Francisco dockworkers who were instrumental in organizing a transnational port shut down. Within the description of the shut down, there is a key paragraph detailing the history of May Day and its ties to workers' rights. It states:

> While widely celebrated outside of the United States, May Day itself was born in Chicago during the struggle for the eight-hour working day. A march by striking workers along Michigan Avenue on May 1, 1886, is widely regarded as the world's first May Day march. In mobilizing for May Day, ILWU leader Clarence Thomas had stated that resolutions against the war were important, but they do not stop wars. "But when you stop the ports, the White House listens and the whole world listens," he said to a gathering in Oakland on April 24. (Lin 3)

Within this short paragraph, there is an attempt to both historicize the labor struggles honored by May Day *and* connect the current labor movement to the anti-war movement. Sharat G. Lin of the San Francisco Independent Media Center is clear throughout his brief documentation of the events in San Francisco that May Day can no longer be just about labor or immigrants, but our current political and economic situation requires these groups to work together. Furthermore, he takes the time to connect to specific histories of the day in order to situate the importance of May Day itself, but then he continues describing the connections being made across different activist groups and their interdependence on one another. By 2008, May Day had become more than a way to rebrand the immigrant or worker. Instead, it became representative of a network of activists working for social justice across the globe.

Although one could argue that May Day itself became the representative umbrella for this shift, I argue that the rallying cry of *¡Sí se puede!* has come to represent the unification of decentralized and multi-tactic organizing. The Spanish phrase translates as "Yes, we can!" and originated in 1972 by United Farm Workers (UFW). Union members, under the leadership of Cesar Chavez, underwent a twenty-five day fast in order to advocate for better working conditions, fair pay, and respectable hours for farm workers. Chavez's non-violent protest strategies mirrored those of civil rights and global leaders such as Rev. Martin Luther King, Jr. and Mahatma Gandhi. Additionally, his protests worked to bring the issue of immigrant labor into the public eye. The link between the protests of UFW, history, and multi-group activism are assembled with *¡Sí se puede!*

The use of the phrase by protesters in 2008 served to not only recall that history, but also to reinforce the deep connections between labor, immigration, and anti-war movements.

The historical and current connections between immigration and labor did not end with Chavez. In fact, one of the central themes of the May Day protest is the reform of both immigration and labor policies to create better, more humane working conditions for people both within and outside the United States. Chavez brought attention to the working conditions of the immigrant farm worker and joined together both immigrants and workers in 1972, and the protesters on May Day continued that tradition. Laury Kenton of the Seattle Independent Media Center describes the protests in the Pacific Northwest. Her account is careful to discuss the close ties between immigration and labor in the United States. She states:

> Today's immigration policies encourage a steady stream of immigrants to work in the nation's factories, fields, and offices. Multinational corporations use immigrants to drive down wages and benefits. When these workers realize that they are being exploited, their vulnerable legal status is used against them. Labor is demanding that wages be determined by the work done, not by the worker's immigration status. Although comprehensive immigration reform isn't on the immediate horizon, the marchers were resolute, many chanting "Sí, se puede!" ("Yes, we can!") as they marched through the streets of Seattle. (Kenton 24)

Kenton's brief description of the power held by multinational companies to influence both the lives of immigrants and U.S. workers alike demonstrates the ways in which immigration and work are deeply connected. However, she does not equate the experiences of immigrants or workers; instead, she assembles the histories and contexts of work without calling immigrants workers or workers citizens. This allows for variation yet connection through difference.

Kenton ends her account with the phrase *¡Sí se puede!* which creates a feeling of hope in an otherwise disheartening narrative of oppression. As a rallying cry, *¡Sí se puede!* becomes a way to join activists together without using brands to elide their differences. For example, the account of the protest in San José, CA, by Carlos Reyes discusses the varied groups and agendas present within the protest. The ending of the rally with a march and chanting of *¡Sí se puede!* shows, for Reyes, the joining of two distinct cultures and sets of concerns during this day of protest. He states:

> On May 1, 1500 youth, families, workers and other community members gathered in east San José to demand legalization, an end to the raids and deportations and respect for human, civil, and labor rights. Speakers at the kick-off rally included members of the community group Voluntarios de la Communidad, who talked about city ID cards and Student Advocates for Higher Education, an organization of undocumented college students. Strengthening Our Lives addressed the

need to register and vote and Mark Silverman, an immigration lawyer, also spoke. After the rally there was a spirited march, chanting, "¡Sí se puede!" and waving Mexican and American flags, through the heart of the Chicano/Mexicano community and on to City Hall in downtown San José. (Reyes 21)

He begins assembling the types of activists and topics of protest involved in the rally, and then ends his piece discussing how the phrase and both American and Mexican flags were present in the march toward City Hall. The joining of two countries' flags, as well as the joining and discussion of multiple groups' concerns are connected by the phrase *¡Sí se puede!* in this account. The idea that "Yes, we can do it!" easily represents the positive messages of all groups without trying to combine all groups into one identity. It is not just those who are branded as American or Mexican, immigrant or worker, activist or student who believe they can make change, but rather all groups and identities have that possibility. The phase *¡Sí se puede!*, then, works to assemble together without representing them as one universal or totalizing identity. It works as a rhetorical assemblage because it places groups together contiguously, not causally or analogously. It is a rallying cry with which all groups, individuals, and positions can identify.

Although the work of the May Day rallies assembles the histories and context of the worker to form a counter-narrative to immigration stories that have circulated in the mainstream media, its traction as a means to re-assemble the term worker is less apparent. In fact, although work and workers are central to the U.S. nation-state, they are often the least discussed or supported political identities. The May Day rallies and their rallying cries of *¡Sí se puede!* were an attempt to globalize the question of labor in the United States, and that seemed to work a bit better. This chapter and its analyses aim to show how assemblage can work as a means to disrupt the kinds of power-laden branding in which bodies are evacuated of meaning, only to become used for nation-building. The proletariat is not always the magic bullet, as Marx once offered. But if we can find a way to reassemble the worker through different stories and alternate contiguities, we may find new forms of praxis wherein assemblage can challenge power instead of serving it.

One way we see this praxis happening is through discussions of non-work and the discussions of unemployment. In fact, Fredric Jameson in his rereading of Marx's *Capital* states:

> Now we can step back and assess the meaning and import of *Capital* as a whole. [It is] about unemployment: its conceptual climax is reached with this proposition that industrial capitalism generates an overwhelming mass of potentially uninvestible capital on one hand, and an ever-increasing mass of unemployed people on the other: a situation we see fully corroborated today in the current crisis of third-stage or finance capital. ("New Reading" 10)

For Jameson, Marx's ur-text is not about surplus value or fetish objects, but instead it is about the masses of unemployed workers versus the mass amounts of capital created in their stead. In other words, late stage or neoliberal capital *must* have high levels of unemployment in order to sustain the larger surplus profits which make it a success. Without those unemployed workers, those profits are compromised, and so is the project of neoliberal capital.

As protests and writing about the surplus of profits housed in the top one percent of the population continue to circulate, direct connections are being made to the extreme and unchanging unemployment numbers across the globe. Instead of disconnected discussions about Wall Street or the bankruptcy of Greece, we are beginning to see a cross-talk amongst advocates for fair labor practices, unemployment rights advocates, and economic watchdogs. The seemingly disjointed narrative, which is often represented through branding, is no longer sufficing. More and more, what is circulating is an intricate narrative of economic reliance on greed and capital excess which happens on the backs of the unemployed. This shift helps to assemble the worker. Much like the NISN circular from the 2008 May Day protest, these narratives link the economic downturn and the role of labor together with our current neoliberal moment. Therefore, "the worker" no longer functions as a mere brand used to join disparate groups, but instead serves as a material entity who can be seen as a functionary of a complex and broken system.

ASSEMBLING BODIES: A CALL FOR RHETORICAL ACTION

Since the U.S. sub-prime mortgage crash in September 2008, and the subsequent market collapse(s) across the globe, work and workers' rights have been on the forefront of public discussions about the economy. Nowhere have they been more present than at what is described as "the ground-zero of the fight": Occupy Wall Street in New York City. This particular located protest did not begin until September 17, 2011, in Liberty Square in Manhattan's Financial district. Since then, the occupation has settled in Zuccotti Park and has satellite occupations throughout the United States. Since the beginning, the world has watched to see the outcome of this protest because although its polished texts seemed typical for anti-corporate activism, the work within the group(s) was much more collective and flexible than most protest movements seen before.

Using the catch-phrase "We are the 99 percent" as a means of grouping all of those who do not identify as corporate power or the super-rich, those who began the Occupy movement did so without clear demands and/or identity markers. This apparent lack of structure from the beginning may seem as if it could lend itself to branding. In some cases, "We are the 99 percent" has been criticized for being white and male in its concerns and commitments.[16] However, I and several other theorists argue that it is the site-specific action that makes Occupy important for advocacy.[17] It is the assembling of many constituencies together, not the branding of them all as "the 99 percent" that is critical to the subversive nature of the Occupy movement.

The work that is done on the ground at Occupy is not about naming and representing particular groups or sub-groups of people. Instead, it is about educating the participants in the historical and local concerns of those who are invested in a similar cause. For example, the foci of the organizers in New York City are different than those in Houston, TX. The reason for the difference is that each location plays a distinct role in U.S. capitalism *and* has its own histories and relationships to gender, race, and class. Much as this book has demonstrated through its examples of specific state and corporate legislation, no matter how unified the U.S. government purports to be, its practices are privatized to individual states, municipalities, and businesses. Therefore, it is not enough for the organizers to say we are resisting capital on a national or global level. Instead, they must make clear how each local site participates in capital practice differently.

Occupy, then, is assembling site-specific occupations under one large organizing umbrella. However, unlike traditional labor and/or cross-border organizing,[18] Occupy is not imposing a series of demands or constraints on each location. Instead, it is up to those collectively at each site to decide what are the most relevant and important calls to resistance at each location. Occupy is attempting to *assemble* a worldwide action without branding the work that they are doing, thus leaving room for each local site to determine their means of resistance. The key to this work is both the assemblage *and* recognizing the centrality of local identities and histories. Therefore, when Occupy attempts to ground discussions of resistance in discussions of local concerns, they come closer to a model of rhetorical action that centers on the assemblage. Instead of branding identities and/or ignoring them altogether in the name of resisting identity politics, Occupy is beginning to assemble bodies who can challenge injustice and fight for more visible and humane labor practices.

As such, Occupy holds the possibility of being an assembled action. It assembles multiple identities and constituencies at each location, and it assembles multiple sites across the globe. If they can find a way to represent their movement without limiting their message to a mere brand—"We are the 99 percent"—Occupy could be seen as a productive site to study rhetorical action that moves away from branding and toward assemblage. As it stands now, however, Occupy is still trying to find that assembled voice. Yes, it does not have a clear spokesperson, but the talking points often read like a traditional white-heteronormative articulation of class, one that does not articulate the differences that gender, immigrant status, race, and labor provide. Instead, by focusing on "the 1 percent versus the 99 percent" many groups are branded within one larger group that is pitted against a universal image of wealth and poverty, which are misleading and easily dismissed.

Therefore, the true challenge for Occupy is to find a way to rhetorically represent itself as the rich assemblage that it is. Finding a way to bring those local assemblages onto the national media scene is the challenge, and if any group is poised to do it, Occupy is. If Occupy does find a way to nationally represent the assemblage, there is hope that a shift can happen in media and legal discourse—one where individuals begin to see them as stakeholders in their local sites and understand how the imperial histories of those sites influence their engagement with capital. However, as long as the media and government dominate discussions through branding, those connections will be difficult to unfold, and branding bodies will continue in the service of neoliberal capital.

NOTES

1. In a right-to-work state, the employer has the right to hire and/or fire employees at will. Workers have little protection in any aspect of their job (hiring, work site, firing). Instead, employers can dismiss employees as they see fit, often without cause, if that is the agreement/contract drawn upon the hiring. In other words, each job and work site has its own agreement about workers' rights. There are not blanket state and/or nationwide protections. The logic is that if employers can set their own terms, they are more likely to create jobs and hire more people, thus creating a state that gives its residents the right to work.

2. Rhetorical action is defined by Rachel Riedner and Kevin Mahoney in *Democracies to Come* as a written or verbal space wherein power can be critiqued and shifted.

3. The latest version of ENDA, H.R. 2015, was put to Congress on April 24, 2007. In this version not only is sexual orientation protected, but also gender identity. This is an important change because the bill, as it reads now, is inclusive of all of those in the GLBT community. It is still being reviewed.

4. This strategy was clearly discussed in Chris Bull's article, in which GLBT activist Frank stated: "DOMA served as a stop-loss order for members of the Senate," says Frank. "In the past they always feared that if they voted for gay rights they would be accused of supporting a much broader gay agenda. When they voted for DOMA and ENDA, they could go home and say, 'Don't tell me I voted for the gay rights agenda. I voted to ban gay marriage.' Members don't have this kind of cover this year."

5. Valentine Moghadam studies Transnational Feminist Networks not as products of transnational/global flows of power, capital, and bodies, but rather as linked processes forging connections between the local and global, as well as between particular economies and the larger power structures which influence them. Moghadam seeks to explore the complex relationships between local and global, state and international, and individual and collective identities and processes forming within these activist groups. Therefore, labor movements are ideal sites for transnational feminist activist work because they begin to look at the structures of production that not only cross international boundaries, but also employ mostly women all over the world.

According to Chandra Talpade Mohanty an awareness of terminology, its legacies, and its uses is needed in order to form meaningful connections and collaborations with activists from around the globe. She analyzes how complex categories of identification, ones that have often been universalized (through humanist analysis) or fragmented (through postmodern discourse), are not fixed globalized or localized tropes, but instead are fluid terms which are influenced by both the micro and macro power structures in which they occur. Mohanty offers transnational feminism as a way to avoid universal or fragmented understandings of identities. Instead of basing solidarity on universal oppression, each woman or group of women should be respected for their differences, but those differences can also link to other differences through analyzing global systems of power—capitalist, political, ideological. Therefore, solidarity becomes a much more complicated term/state to achieve because it cannot rely on universals, nor can it be avoided by believing that particular experiences can find no common ground between them.

Mohanty, like Moghadam, is not asserting the ease of finding common ground though difference. Instead, she is claiming the necessity of these kinds of focused coalitions in order to create meaningful change in the age of global capitalism. Therefore, instead of relying on organizing brands, such as woman, worker, and family, Mohanty is asserting that activists need to do the difficult work of critical analysis and listening in order to understand how women, workers, and families are different depending on their location of origin. Then, from those critical differences, they can begin to find similar oppressions, legacies, and/or power structures which can form the basis of their coalition.

6. As of 2012, the Human Resource Counsel (H.R.C) report on GLBT friendly workplaces gives Apple a "zero" in engaging with activist or public support of GLBT causes.

7. For Duggan, homonationalism is the rise of the white-gay-male as an acceptable and welcomed category of capitalist power. She sees this figure as central to neoliberalism, and as such the gay-white-upper-middle-class male is often a site of power in government, marketing, and media.

8. Michel Foucault in *History of Sexuality Vol. 1* discusses how in the nineteenth century homosexuals (those accused of sodomy) became nothing more than the act of sodomy. The whole of their history, identity, and legal status was defined by the *action* of sodomy rather than other identificatory markers.

9. "a) NONPRIVATE CONDUCT. – Nothing in this Act shall be constructed to prohibit a covered entity from enforcing rules regarding nonprivate sexual conduct, if the rules of conduct are designed for, and uniformly applied to all individuals."

10. Most recent May Day observances date back to the early twentieth century when the Industrial Workers of the World (IWW or Wobblies) organized massive strikes and boycotts in order to protest the ghastly hours and working conditions of industrial factory work.

11. The Workers and Families party is an active political party who has its roots in the Socialist Party of the U.S. However, unlike other offshoots of the Socialist Party (like the Wobblies) this party creates alliances with capital and other political parties in order to get agendas pushed through and candidates elected. Yes, work is central to their platform, but changing out the economic and political system in the name of Workers is not.

12. Max Weber's *Protestant Ethic and the Spirit of Capitalism* is the most famous articulation of this connection. However many others have noted the United States's particular connection between capital and Protestant ethics—hard work, individualism—as central to the move to neoliberalism today.

13. Jefferson is drawing directly from British philosopher John Locke, who stated if men had their own self-interest (translated into their own private property) to guide them, they would act honorably in order to protect and manage their own land.

14. According to Jennifer Hyndman: "the discourse of 'UN humanism' is analyzed, noting a long-standing tension between culture as shared humanity and culture as a pivotal basis of difference. Drawing on current research relating to UNHCR's gender policies and on initiatives against violence towards refugee women in camps, the implications of overarching frameworks which attend to gender and cultural differences are discussed. Strategies to avoid authenticating or fixing categories of difference, on the one hand, and to avoid treating gender and culture as simply variables,

on the other, are proposed in the context of emerging transnational feminist practices. Transnational approaches point to important interventions which may serve to unravel the dominant discourses of UN humanism and vulnerable groups that continue to organize UN refugee and humanitarian operations today."

15. The ISG's rhetoric also draws upon the work of the Wobblies post–WWI who fought for labor rights and anti-monopoly laws, as well as civil rights discourses from the 1950s to the 1960s that stressed non-violence and peaceful protest through education.

16. Linda Alcoff has written about the gender and safety education taking place in Zuccotti Park, and I was contacted by Occupy Houston to discuss feminism within their camp in an effort to address what they perceived as a gender disparity in their organizing.

17. Jodi Dean, Lisa Duggan, Linda Alcoff, and Rosemary Hennessy all endorse the process based organizing and education that happens on-site at Occupy. Therefore, Occupy can be seen as a productive space for education and resistance through individual and communal exchange.

18. The labor solidarity against Levi-Strauss and Co. in the 1990s and the Basmati Rice Collective in the 2000s both organized around a particular issue, but they used grassroots education and discussion to forward their causes.

Bibliography

"About." *Occupy Wallst.com*. http://occupywallst.org/about. Web. 1 May 2012.

Achbar, Mark and Jennifer Abbot, and Joel Bakan, directors. *The Corporation*. Vancouver, BC: Big Picture Productions, 2003. Film.

Agamben, Giorgio. *Homo Sacer: Sovereign Power and Bare Life*. Palo Alto, CA: Stanford UP, 1998. Print.

Ahmed, Sara. "Affective Economies." *Social Text* 22.2 (Summer 2004): 117–39. Print.

———. *The Cultural Politics of Emotion*. New York: Routledge, 2004. Print.

———. *Strange Encounters: Embodied Others in Post-Coloniality*. New York: Routledge, 2000. Print.

Alexander. M. Jacqui. *Pedagogies of Crossing: Meditation of Feminisms, Sexual Politics, Memory, and The Sacred*. Durham, NC: Duke UP, 2005. Print.

Anonymous. "A May Day fight for workers' rights." *Industrial Worker*. Philadelphia: May 2006. Vol. 103, Iss. 5. 7. Print.

———. "Yesterday We Marched, Today We Act, Tomorrow We Vote." *La Prensa San Diego*. San Diego: Apr 28, 2006. Vol. 30, Iss. 17. 4.

Arvidsson, Adam. *Brands: Meaning and Value in Media Culture*. New York, Routledge, 2006. Print.

Associated Press. "Afghan shootings suspect set to face charges in US, says expert." *The Guardian*. 18 March 2012. http://www.guardian.co.uk/world/2012/mar/18/afghanistan-shootings-suspect-charges?CMP=twt_fd. Web. 19 March 2012.

———. "Hundreds of illegal immigrants are seized in sweep." *St. Louis Post-Dispatch*. St. Louis, MO: Jun 18, 2006. A.4. Print.

———. "LA man faces charges of molesting boys in Thailand." *Los Angeles Times*. 18 May 2006. A8. Print.

Bacon, David. "Justice deported." *People's Weekly World*. New York: Dec 23–Dec 29, 2006. Vol. 21, Iss. 28, 13. Print.

Banjaree, Payal. "Indian IT Workers in the US: Flexible Hiring and Immigrants' Experiences of Contract Work under the H-1B Visa." Unpublished conference paper. 2 June 2006. Lecture.

Bauerlin, Monika and Clara Jeffery. "All Work and No Pay: The Great Work Speed-up." *Mother Jones*. July/August 2011. http://motherjones.com/politics/2011/06/speed-up-american-workers-long-hours. Web. 28 September 2011.

Berlant, Lauren. "The Epistemology of State Emotion." *Dissent in Dangerous Times*. Austin Sarat, ed. Ann Arbor, MI: U of Michigan P, 2005. 46–79. Print.

———. *The Queen of America Goes to Washington City: Essays on Sex and Citizenship*. Durham, NC: Duke UP, 1997. Print.

Bernstein, Nina. "Companies use Immigration Crackdown to Turn a Profit." *The New York Times*. 29 September 2011. http://www.nytimes.com/2011/09/29/world/asia/getting-tough-on-immigrants-to-turn-a-profit.html. Web. 29 September 2011.

Bernstein, Jake. "Lamar's Alien Agenda: Why is Mr. Smith Still in Washington?" *The Texas Observer* 94.20 (October 25, 2002): 4. Print.

Brah, Avtar. *Cartographies of Diaspora: Contesting Identities*. London: Routledge, 1996. Print.

Braziel, Janna Evans. "Haiti, Guantánamo, and the 'One Indispensable Nation': U.S. Imperialism, 'Apparent States,' and Postcolonial Problematics of Sovereignty." *Cultural Critique* 64 (Autumn 2006): 127–160. Print.

131

Brown, Wendy. "Neoliberalism and the End of Liberal Democracy." *Theory and Event* 7.1 (2003). Web. http://muse.jhu.edu.ezproxy.lib.uh.edu/journals/theory_and_event/v007/7.1brown.html.

Burke, Kenneth. *A Rhetoric of Motives.* Berkeley, CA: University of California Press, 1969.

Bush, President George W. "President Discusses War on Terrorism. In Address to the Nation, Atlanta, GA. 8 November 2001." Press Release. Web. http://www.whitehouse.gov/news/releases/2001/11/20011108-13.html. 26 June 2008.

———. "Radio Address to the Nation. 15 September 2001." Press Release. Web. http://www.whitehouse.gov/news/releases/2001/09/20010915.html. 26 June 2008.

"Bush's 'Secret' Detainees." *Wall Street Journal.* New York, NY: Aug 8, 2002. A.12. Print.

Butler, Judith. "Is Kinship Always Already Heterosexual?" *Going Public: Feminism and the Shifting Boundaries of the Private Sphere.* Eds. Joan W. Scott and Debra Keates. Urbana, IL: U of Illinois P, 2004. 123–50. Print.

"Buyers Guide—Apple." *Human Rights Counsel.com.* Web. http://www.hrc.org/apps/buyersguide/profile.php?orgid=1326#.T6AEj7_R0eN. 1 May 2012.

California State Legislature. "Proposition 187 (a.k.a The Save Our State Initiative.)" 1994. Web. http://www.americanpatrol.com/REFERENCE/prop187text.html. 26 June 2008.

Camacho, Alicia Schmidt. "Hailing the Twelve Million: U.S. Immigration Policy, Deportation, and the Imaginary of Lawful Violence." *Social Text 105* 28.4 (Winter 2010): 1–24. Print.

Carr, Rebecca. "Courts restore detainee rights." *The Atlanta Journal-Constitution.* Atlanta, GA: Dec 19, 2003. A.1. Print.

Clough, Patricia Ticineto and Craig Willse. "Gendered Security/National Security: Political Branding and Population Racism." *Social Text 105* 28.4 (Winter 2010): 45–63. Print.

Cohen, Lisbeth. *A Consumer's Republic: The Politics of Mass Consumption in Post War America.* New York: Vintage, 2003. Print.

Dam, Bette. "'Why did they not stop the killings?'" *Salon: Global Post.* 15 March 2012. http://www.salon.com/2012/03/15/why_did_they_not_stop_the_killings. Web. 19 March 2012.

Danilov, Dan P. "Highlights of New 1996 U.S. Immigration Laws." *Northwest Asian Weekly.* Seattle, WA (22 Nov 1996): 12. Print.

Dean, Jodi. *Democracy and Other Neoliberal Fantasies: Communicative Capitalism and Leftist Politics.* Durham, NC: Duke UP, 2009. Print.

———. "Roundtable: Three Theses on Neoliberalism (or Contestants, but not Entrepreneurs)." *American Political Science Association.* Septermber 2011. Lecture.

DeChaine, D. Robert. "Ethos in a Bottle: Corporate Social Responsibility and Humanitarian Doxa." *The Megarhetorics of Global Development.* Rebecca Dingo and J. Blake Scott, eds. Pittsburgh, PA: U of Pittsburgh P, 2012. 75–100. Print.

Defense of Marriage Act. Pub. L. No. 104–199, 21 Sept. 1996. Stat. 110.2419. Print.

DeGette, Cara. "We are human beings." *Colorado Springs Independent.* Colorado Springs: May 4–May 10, 2006. Vol. 14, Iss. 18. 8. Print.

DeLanda, Miguel. *A New Philosophy of Society: Assemblage Theory and Social Complexity.* London: Continuum, 2006. Print.

Deleuze, Gilles. "Postscript on the Societies of Control." *October* 59 (Winter 1992): 3–7. Print.

Dingo, Rebecca. "Linking Transnational Logics: A Feminist Rhetorical Analysis of Public Policy Networks." *College English* 70.4 (May 2008): 482–97. Print.

———. *Networking Arguments: Rhetoric, Transnational Feminism, and Public Policy.* Pittsburgh, PA: U of Pittsburgh, 2012. Print.

Dingo, Rebecca and J. Blake Scott. *The Megarhetorics of Global Development.* Pittsburgh, PA: U of Pittsburgh P, 2012. Print.

Duany, Andres, Elixabeth Plater-Zyberk, and Jeff Speck. *Suburban Nation: The Rise of Sprawl and the Decline of the American Dream*. New York. North Point Press, 2000. Print.

Duggan, Lisa. "Feeling Neoliberal: Homonormative Desires, Imperial Dreams." University of Houston. Houston, TX. 27 April 2012. Lecture.

———. *The Twilight of Equality?: Neoliberalism, Cultural Politics, and the Attack on Democracy*. Boston, MA: Beacon Press, 2004. Print.

Edbauer, Jenny. "Executive Overspill: Affective Bodies, Intensity, and Bush-in-Relation." *Postmodern Culture* 15.1 (2004). Web. http://muse.jhu.edu.libezproxy2.syr.edu/journals/postmodern_culture/v015/15.1edbauer.html. 30 June 2008.

———. "Unframing Models of Public Distribution: From Rhetorical Situation to Rhetorical Ecologies." *Rhetoric Society Quarterly* 35.4 (Fall 2005): 5–24. Print.

Edelman, Lee. *No Escape: Queer Theory and the Death Drive*. Durham, NC: Duke UP, 2004. Print.

"Filipino Workers join May Day March for amnesty." *The Filipino Express*. Jersey City: May 13, 2001. Vol. 15, Iss. 19. 2. Print.

Finley, Bruce. "International gangs spread Of 375 arrests in past 2 weeks" *Denver Post*. Denver, CO: Mar 12, 2006. C02. Print.

Forden, Geoffrey. "Protecting Us Without Tainting the Constitution." *Boston Globe*. Boston, MA: Jul 17, 2004. A11. Print.

Foucault, Michel. *History of Sexuality Vol. 1: An Introduction*. New York: Vintage, 1990. Print.

———. "On Governmentality." *Ideology and Consciousness* 6 (1979): 5–26. Print.

Frank, Thomas. *What's the Matter with Kansas?: How They Won the Heart of America*. New York: Holt, 2005. Print.

Gale, Daryl. "Islam Inside." *City Paper*. Philadelphia, PA: Jul 4, 2002. 893. 15. Print.

Gates, Henry Louis. *The Signifying Monkey: A Theory of African-American Literary Criticism*. Oxford, UK: Oxford University Press, 1988.

Gobé, Marc. *Citizen Brand: 10 Commandments for Transforming Brands in a Consumer Democracy*. New York: Allworth Press, 2002. Print.

Greenhouse, Linda. "Justices Decline Terrorism Case of a U.S. Citizen." *New York Times*. New York, NY: Apr 4, 2006. A1. Print.

Hage, Ghassan. *White Nation: Fantasies of White Supremacy in a Multicultural Society*. Annandale, NSW: Pluto Press, 1998. Print.

Haynes, William. "Enemy Combatants." *Council on Foreign Relations*. 12 December 2002. Web. http://www.cfr.org/publication.html?id=5312. 30 June 2008.

Healy, Patrick O'gilfoil. "A Gang Sweep With a Difference." *New York Times*. New York, NY: Mar 27, 2005. LI.1. Print.

Hennessy, Rosemary. "Revisioning Class and the Value of a Second Skin." *Graduate Student Literature Conference*. University of Houston. Houston, TX. 31 March 2012. Lecture.

Hesford, Wendy. "*Kairos* and the Geopolitical Rhetorics of Global Sex Work and Video Advocacy." *Just Advocacy? Women's Human Rights, Transnational Feminisms, and the Politics of Representation*. Eds. Wendy S. Hesford and Wendy Kozol. New Brunswick, NJ: Rutgers UP, 2005. 146–72. Print.

———. *Spectacular Rhetorics: Human Rights Visions, Recognitions, Feminisms*. Durham, NC: Duke UP, 2011. Print.

Hin, Lee Siu. "May Day 2008 Call to Action." *May Day 2008 International Workers Day and Mobilization to Support Immigrant Rights!: Reports from Around the World*. Ed Lee Siu Hin. *National Immigrant Solidarity Network*. Web. http://www.immigrantsolidarity.org/Documents/MayDay08Reports.pdf. 26 June 2008.

Hirschkorn, Phil. "Jose Padilla's Mental State at Issue." *CBS News*. 24 February 2007. Web.http://www.cbsnews.com/stories/2007/02/24/cbsnews_investigates/main2510272.shtml. 26 June 2008.

Hong, Grace Kyungwon. "Existentially Surplus: Women of Color Feminism and the Crises of Capitalism." *GLQ: A Journal of Lesbian and Gay Studies* 18.1 (2012): 87–106. Print.

Ifill, Sherrilyn A. "Questioning Ashcroft." *Afro-American Red Star*. Washington, D.C.: Sep 20, 2002. 111.5. A7. Print.

Illegal Immigration Reform and Immigrant Responsibility Act of 1996. Pub.L. 104–208. 30 Sept. 1996. Stat. 3009–546. Print.

Immigration and Customs Enforcement Agency. "40 Salinas Residents Arrested in ICE Effort Targeting Criminal Alien Sex Offenders." Press Release. 31 August 2006. Web. http://www.ice.gov/pi/news/newsreleases/chapters/060831Salinas.htm. 26 June 2008.

———. "ICE comments on Houston man sentenced to 30 years in prison for producing, distributing and possessing nearly 4,000 images of child porn." Press Release. 15 December 2006. Web. http://www.ice.gov/pi/news/newsreleases/chapters/061215houston.htm. 26 June 2008.

———. "Operation Predator." Fact Sheet. 25 January 2008. Web.http://www.ice.gov/pi/news/factsheets/070607operationpredator.htm. 26 June 2008.

———. "U.S. Uncovers Large-Scale Identity Theft Scheme Used By Illegal Aliens to Gain Employment at Nationwide Meat Processor." Press Release. 13 December 2006. Web. http://www.ice.gov/pi/news/newsreleases/chapters/061213dc.htm. 26 June 2008.

Jagoda, Patrick. "Terror Networks and the Aesthetics of Interconnection." *Social Text* 105 28.4 (Winter 2010): 65–89. Print.

Jakobsen, Janet R. "Can Homosexuals End Western Civilization as We Know it?: Family Values in a Global Economy." *Queer Globalizations: Citizenship and the Afterlife of Colonialism*. Arnaldo Cruz-Malavé and Martin Mansalan, eds. New York: New York UP, 2002. 49–70. Print.

———. "Perverse Justice." *GLQ: A Journal of Lesbian and Gay Studies* 18.1 (2012): 19–45. Print."Jobs at Apple." http://www.apple.com/jobs/us/benefits.html. Web. 11 June 2012.

Jameson, Fredric. "A New Reading of *Capital*." *Mediations* 25.1 (Fall 2010): 5–14. www.mediationsjournal.org/a-new-reading-of-capital. Web.

Johnson, Kevin and John Diamond. "Al-Qaeda is active in USA, Ashcroft warns." *USA TODAY*. McLean, VA: Jul 12, 2002. A02. Print.

Joshi, Monika. "Immigrants march together on May Day." *India in New York*. New York, NY: May 4, 2001. 4.44. 8. Print.

Kaplan, Amy. "Homeland Insecurities: Reflections on Language and Space." *Radical History Review* 85 (Winter 2003): 82–93. Print.

Keillor, Garrison. "Stating the Obvious." *Salon.com*. Web. 17 March 2007.

Kenton, Laury. "Untitled." *May Day 2008 International Workers Day and Mobilization to Support Immigrant Rights!: Reports from Around the World*. Ed Lee Hin Siu. *National Immigrant Solidarity Network*. Web. http://www.immigrantsolidarity.org/Documents/MayDay08Reports.pdf. 26 June 2008. 23–24.

Kienzel, Olivia. "One Nation Under Surveillance" *Santa Barbara Independent*. Santa Barbara, CA: Feb 13, 2003 17.846. 19. Print.

Klein, Naomi. *No Logo*. New York: Picador, 2000. Print.

———. *The Shock Doctrine: The Rise of Disaster Capitalism*. New York: Picador, 2008. Print.

Koch, Wendy. "Child porn suspects include a teacher." *USA Today*. McLean, VA: Mar 17, 2006. A.3. Print.

Laura. Phone Message. 8 December 2006. *Immigrant Solidarity Group*. Audio File.

"Letters." *The Christian Science Monitor*. Boston, MA: Feb 22, 2007. 08. Print.

"Letter to the Editor: Jitters in America: The Case of the 'Dirty Bomb.'" *New York Times*. New York, NY: Jun 12, 2002. 28. Print.

Lin, Sharat G. "May Day Revival on Three Fronts: Labor, Immigrant, and Antiwar." *May Day 2008 International Workers Day and Mobilization to Support Immigrant*

Rights!: Reports from Around the World. Ed Lee Hin Siu. *National Immigrant Solidarity Network.* Web. http://www.immigrantsolidarity.org/Documents/May-Day08Reports.pdf. 26 June 2008. 3–4.

Lindsley, Syd. "The Gendered Assault on Immigrants." *Policing the National Body: Race, Gender, and Criminalization.* Eds. Jael Silliman and Anannya Bhattacharjee. Cambridge, MA: South End Press. 2002. Print.

Liptak, Adam. "Accord Suggests U.S. Prefers to Avoid Courts." *New York Times.* New York, NY: Jul 16, 2002. A14. Print.

———. "In Terror Cases, Administration Sets Own Rules." *New York Times.* New York, NY: Nov 27, 2005. A1. Print.

Lury, Celia. *Brands: The Logos of the Global Economy.* New York: Routledge, 2004. Print.

Mason, Jeff and Alister Bull. "Osama bin Laden's Wife Not Killed in Raid." *Reuters.* 3 May 2011. Web. http://www.reuters.com/article/2011/05/02/us-binladen-usa-wife-idUSTRE7416G220110502. 25 September 2011.

Massumi, Brian. "Fear (The Spectrum Said)." *Positions* 13.1 (2005): 31–48. Print.

———. *Parables for the Virtual: Movement, Affect, Sensation*: Raleigh, NC: Duke UP, 2002. Print.

Merpu Roa. "Filipinos join big May Day NY rally." *The Filipino Express.* Jersey City: May 8–May 14, 2006. 20.19. 31–3. Print.

"Mexican Leader Criticized for his comments on Blacks." *CNN.com.* 15 May 2005. Web. http://www.cnn.com/2005/US/05/14/fox.jackson. 26 June 2008.

Mohanty, Chandra Talpade. "US Empire and the Project of Women's Studies: Stories of Citizenship, Complicity and Dissent." *Gender, Place and Culture* 13.2 (February 2006): 7–20. Print.

"National Institutes of Health." Pub. L. 103–43. 107 stat. 122 (1993). Print.

Ong, Aihwa. *Neoliberalism as Exception: Mutations in Citizenship and Sovereignty.* Durham, NC: Duke UP, 2007. Print.

"Osama Bin Laden Killed in Pakistan." *AlJazeer.net.* 2 May 2011. Web. http://english.aljazeera.net/news/americas/2011/05/2011522132275789.html. 19 September 2011.

"Our Opinions: Constitutional rights not optional." *The Atlanta Journal-Constitution.* Atlanta, GA: Nov 26, 2003. A16. Print.

Patton, Cindy. *Inventing AIDS.* New York: Routledge, 2001. Print.

Puar, Jasbir K. "Queer Times, Queer Assemblages." *Social Text* 84–85. 3–4 (November 2005): 121–39. Print.

———. *Terrorist Assemblages: Homonationalism in Queer Times.* Durham, NC: Duke UP, 2007. Print.

Puar, Jasbir K. and Amit Rai. "Monster, Terrorist, Fag: The War on Terrorism and the Production of Docile Patriots." *Social Text 72* 20.3 (Fall 2002): 117–48. Print.

Reddy, Chandan. *Freedom with Violence: Race, Sexuality, and the US State.* Durham, NC: Duke UP, 2011. Print.

Reyes, Carlos. "May 1 Immigrant Rights March." *May Day 2008 International Workers Day and Mobilization to Support Immigrant Rights!: Reports from Around the World.* ed. Lee Hin Siu. *National Immigrant Solidarity Network.* Web. http://www.immigrantsolidarity.org/Documents/MayDay08Reports.pdf. 26 June 2008. 21–2.

Richey, Warren. "Legal landmines emerge in 'dirty bomber' case." *The Christian Science Monitor.* Boston, MA: Aug 31, 2006. 01. Print.

Riedner, Rachel. "Local and Global Identification and Literacy: What is to Be Done?" *Present Tense: A Journal for Rhetoric and Society.* http://www.presenttensejournal.org. Web. Forthcoming.

———. *Responsibility at a Distance.* Unpublished Manuscript. Print.

Riedner, Rachel and Kevin Mahoney. *Democracies to Come: Rhetorical Action, Neoliberalism, and Communities of Resistance.* Lanham, MD: Lexington Books, 2008. Print.

Schabner, Dean and Karen Travers. "Osama Bin Laden Killed: 'Justice is Done,' President Says." *ABCNews.com*. 01 May 2011. Web. http://abcnews.go.com/Blotter/osama-bin-laden-killed/story?id=13505703. 19 September 2011.

Scherer, Ron and Alexandra Marks. "Gangs, prison: Al Qaeda breeding grounds?" *Christian Science Monitor*. Boston, MA: Jun 14, 2002. 02. Print.

Scott, J. Blake. "Kairos as Indeterminate Risk Management: The Pharmaceutical Industry's Response to Bioterrorism." *Quarterly Journal of Speech* 92 (2006): 115–43. Print.

Shirazi, Nima. "American Morlocks: Monsters of a murderous Afghan policy." *Salon.com*. 14 March 2012. Web. http://www.salon.com/2012/03/14/american_morlocks_monsters_of_a_murderous_afghan_policy. 19 March 2012.

"Sketches get interest of conspiracy buffs." *Houston Chronicle*. Houston, TX: Jul 7, 2002. 2.

Somerville, Sibohan. "Notes toward a Queer History of Naturalization." *American Quarterly* 57.3 (2005): 659–75. Print.

Stewart, Kathleen. *Ordinary Affects*. Durham, NC: Duke UP, 2007. Print.

Stob, Paul. "Kenneth Burke, John Dewey, and the Pursuit of the Public." *Philosophy and Rhetoric* 38.3 (2005): 226–47. Print.

Tackett, Michael. "U.S. takes unusual course, calls citizen a combatant." *Chicago Tribune*. Chicago, IL: Jun 11, 2002. 1. Print.

Thermos, Wendy. "Auction Director Held in Probe." *Los Angeles Times*. Los Angeles, CA: Jun 4, 2005. B4. Print.

"Three Years Late." *The Washington Post*. Washington, D.C.: Nov 23, 2005. A18. Print.U.S. Constitution. Art. IV. Sec. 1. Print.

United States. Cong. Senate. 108th Congress, 1st Session. *H.J. Res. 56* "Federal Marriage Amendment." 21 May 2003. Print.

———. *S. 151* "Prosecutorial Remedies and Other Tools to end the Exploitation of Children Today Act of 2003. (a.k.a. PROTECT Act)." 7 January 2003. Print.

United States. Cong. Senate. 109th Congress, 2nd Session. *H.R. 4437* "Border Protection, Antiterrorism, and Illegal Immigration Control Act of 2005." 17 Dec. 2005. Print.

"United States HIV Immigration and Travel Policy." *Act Up: AIDS Coalition to Unleash Power*. Web. http://www.actupny.org/actions/Immigration.html. 26 June 2008.

Uniting and Strengthening America by Providing Appropriate Tools Required to Intercept and Obstruct Terrorism (USA Patriot Act) Act of 2001. Pub. L. no. 107–56 (2001). Print.

"Usama Bin Laden Killed in Firefight with U.S. Special Ops Team in Pakistan." *Fox-News.com* 02 May 2011. Web. http://www.foxnews.com/us/2011/05/01/usama-bin-laden-dead-say-sources. 19 September 2011.

"US Tries to Block Release of Bin Laden Images." *Al Jazeera.Net*. 28 September 2011. Web.http://english.aljazeera.net/news/americas/2011/09/201192855011244268.html. 28 September 2011.

Watney, Simon. "The Spectacle of AIDS." *AIDS: Cultural Analysis/Cultural Activism*. Ed. Douglas Crimp. Cambridge, MA: MIT UP, 1988. 71–86. Print.

Weaver, Jay and Lisa Arthur. "Timeline: The Jose Padilla Case." *Miami Herald.com*. 2007. Web. http://www.miamiherald.com/multimedia/news/padilla. 26 June 2008.

Weinstein, Adam. "The Trayvon Martin Killing, Explained." *Mother Jones*. 18 March 2012. Web. http://m.motherjones.com/politics/2012/03/what-happened-trayvon-martin-explained. 19 March 2012.

Weiser, Benjamin and Dana Canedy. "Lawyer Plans Challenge To Detention of Suspect."New York, NY: *New York Times*. Jun 12, 2002. A24. Print.

Weisman, Jonathan, Debbie Howlett and Dave Moniz. "American Terror Suspect is Not Unique." *USA TODAY*. McLean, VA: Jun 11, 2002. A01. Print.

Williams, Raymond. *Marxism and Literature*. Oxford: Oxford University Press, 1977. Print.

Wilson, Scott and Craig Whitlock, and William Branigin. "Osama bin Laden killed in U.S. Raid, Buried at Sea." *The Washington Post.com.* 2 May 2011. Web.http://www.washingtonpost.com/national/osama-bin-laden-killed-in-us-raid-buried-at-sea/2011/05/02/AFx0yAZF_story.html. 19 September 2011.

Index

About the Author

Jennifer Wingard is assistant professor of rhetoric, composition, and pedagogy and a faculty affiliate to the women's studies program at the University of Houston. Over the past five years, she helped design and implement the new PhD concentration in rhetoric, composition, and pedagogy. She specializes in twentieth-century rhetorical theory, transnational feminist theory, and materialist theories of teaching English in the corporate university. Her scholarship focuses on the impact of global neoliberal economics on local civic discourses, and she has been published in *Reflections*, *Journal of Advanced Composition* (*JAC*), and other interdisciplinary edited collections. She is currently working on her second book, tentatively titled *No Zoning! Houston, TX: The Rhetoric of the Neoliberal City*.

Edwards Brothers Malloy
Thorofare, NJ USA
April 22, 2013